172833

Mit        Mitchell, Richard

           Less than words
           can say

Less
Than
Words
Can
Say

# Less Than Words Can Say

By Richard Mitchell

Little, Brown and Company

Boston   Toronto

COPYRIGHT © 1979 BY RICHARD MITCHELL

FIRST EDITION

LIBRARY OF CONGRESS CATALOGING IN PUBLICATION DATA

Mitchell, Richard.
    Less than words can say.

    1. Language and languages. 2. Language arts—
United States. 3. English language—Usage.
4. Thought and thinking. I. Title.
P112.M5      301.2'1      79–15484
ISBN 0–316–57506–2

*172833*

Designed by Janis Capone

BP

*Published simultaneously in Canada
by Little, Brown & Company (Canada) Limited*

PRINTED IN THE UNITED STATES OF AMERICA

# Less
# Than
# Words
# Can
# Say

# Foreword

A colleague sent me a questionnaire. It was about my
goals in teaching, and it asked me to assign values to a
number of beautiful and inspiring goals. I was told that
the goals were pretty widely shared by professors all
around the country.

Many years earlier I had returned a similar questionnaire, because the man who sent it had promised, in
writing, to "analize" my "input." That seemed appropriate, so I put it in. But he didn't do as he had promised,
and I had lost all interest in questionnaires.

This one intrigued me, however, because it was lofty.
It spoke of a basic appreciation of the liberal arts, a
critical evaluation of society, emotional development,
creative capacities, students' self-understanding, moral
character, interpersonal relations and group participa-
tion, and general insight into the knowledge of a discipline. Unexceptionable goals, every one. Yet it seemed to

me, on reflection, that they were none of my damned business. It seemed possible, even likely, that some of those things might flow from the study of language and literature, which *is* my damned business, but they also might not. Some very well-read people lack moral character and show no creative capacities at all, to say nothing of self-understanding or a basic appreciation of the liberal arts. So, instead of answering the questionnaire, I paid attention to its language; and I began by asking myself how "interpersonal relations" were different from "relations." Surely, I thought, our relations with domestic animals and edible plants were not at issue here; why specify them as "interpersonal"? And how else can we "participate" but in groups? I couldn't answer.

I asked further how a "basic" appreciation was to be distinguished from some other kind of appreciation. I recalled that some of my colleagues were in the business of *teaching* appreciation. It seemed all too possible that they would have specialized their labors, some of them teaching elementary appreciation and others intermediate appreciation, leaving to the most exalted members of the department the senior seminars in advanced appreciation, but even that didn't help with basic appreciation. It made about as much sense as blue appreciation.

As I mulled this over, my eye fell on the same word in the covering letter, which said, "We would appreciate having you respond to these items." Would they, could they, "basically appreciate" having me respond to these items? Yes, I think they could. And what is the appropriate response to an item? Would it be a basic response?

Suddenly I couldn't understand anything. I noticed, as though for the first time, that the covering letter promised "to complete the goals and objectives aspect of the report." What is a goals aspect? An objectives aspect? How do you complete an aspect? How seriously could I take a mere aspect, when my mind was beguiled by the possibility of a basic aspect? Even of a basic goals and basic objectives basic aspect?

After years of fussing about the pathetic, baffled language of students, I realized that it was not in their labored writings that bad language dwelt. *This,* this inane gabble, this was bad language. Evil language. Here was a man taking the public money for the work of his mind and darkening counsel by words without understanding.

Words never fail. We hear them, we read them; they enter into the mind and become part of us for as long as we shall live. Who speaks reason to his fellow men bestows it upon them. Who mouths inanity disorders thought for all who listen. There must be some minimum allowable dose of inanity beyond which the mind cannot remain reasonable. Irrationality, like buried chemical waste, sooner or later must seep into all the tissues of thought.

This man had offered me inanity. I had almost seized it. If I told you that this little book would provide *you* with general insight into the knowledge of a discipline, would you read on? If so, then you had *better* read on, for you are in danger. People all around you are offering inanity, and you are ready to seize it, like any well-behaved American consumer dutifully swallowing the best advertised pill. You are, in a certain sense, unconscious.

Language is the medium in which we are conscious. The speechless beasts are aware, but they are not conscious. To be conscious is to "know with" something, and a language of some sort is the device with which we know. More precisely, it is the device with which we *can* know. We don't have to. We can, if we please, speak of general insight into the knowledge of a discipline and forgo knowing.

Consciousness has degrees. We can be wide awake or sound asleep. We can be anesthetized. He is not fully conscious who can speak lightly of such things as basic appreciations and general insights into the knowledge of a discipline. He wanders in the twilight sleep of knowing where insubstantial words, hazy and disembodied, have fled utterly from things and ideas. His is an attractive world, dreamy and undemanding, a Lotus-land of dozing addicts. They blow a little smoke our way. It smells good. Suddenly and happily we realize that our creative capacities and self-understanding yearn after basic appreciations and general insights. We nod, we drowse, we fall asleep.

I am trying to stay awake.

# 1

# The Worm
# in the Brain

There's an outrageous but entertaining assertion about language and the human brain in Carl Sagan's *Dragons of Eden*. It is possible, Sagan says, to damage the brain in precisely such a way that the victim will lose the ability to understand the passive or to devise prepositional phrases or something like that. No cases are cited, unfortunately — it would be fun to chat with some victim — but the whole idea is attractive, because if it were true it would explain many things. In fact, I can think of no better way to account for something that happened to a friend of mine — and probably to one of yours too.

He was an engaging chap, albeit serious. We did some work together — well, not exactly work, committee stuff — and he used to send me a note whenever there was to be a meeting. Something like this: "Let's meet next Monday at two o'clock, OK?" I was always delighted to read such perfect prose.

Unbeknownst to us all, however, something was happening in that man's brain. Who can say what? Perhaps a sleeping genetic defect was stirring, perhaps some tiny creature had entered in the porches of his ear and was gnawing out a home in his cranium. We'll never know. Whatever it was, it had, little by little, two effects. At one and the same time, he discovered in himself the yearning to be an assistant dean pro tem, and he began to lose the power of his prose. Ordinary opinion, up to now, has always held that one of these things, either one, was the cause of the other. Now we can at last guess the full horror of the truth. *Both* are symptoms of serious trouble in the brain.

Like one of these Poe characters whose friends are all doomed, I watched, helpless, the inexorable progress of the disease. Gradually but inevitably my friend was being eaten from within. In the same week that saw his application for the newly created post of assistant dean pro tem, he sent me the following message: "This is to inform you that there'll be a meeting next Monday at 2:00." Even worse, much worse, was to come.

A week or so later it was noised about that he would indeed take up next semester a new career as a high-ranking assistant dean pro tem. I was actually writing him a note of congratulation when the campus mail brought me what was to be his last announcement of a meeting of our committee. Hereafter he would be frying fatter fish, but he wanted to finish the business at hand. His note read: "Please be informed that the Committee on Memorial Plaques will meet on Monday at 2:00."

I walked slowly to the window, his note in my hand, and stared for a while at the quad. The oak trees there had been decimated not long before by a leak in an underground gas line. The seeping poison had killed their very roots, but they had at least ended up as free firewood for the faculty. Pangloss might have been right, after all, and, calamity that it was, this latest message spared me the trouble of writing the congratulatory note and even afforded me a glimpse of a remarkably attractive young lady straying dryad-fashion through the surviving oaks. Things balance out.

You would think, wouldn't you, that the worm or whatever had at last done its work, that the poor fellow's Hydification was complete and his destruction assured. No. It is a happy mercy that most of us cannot begin to imagine the full horror of these ravaging disorders. To this day that man still sends out little announcements and memos about this and that. They begin like this: "You are hereby informed . . ." Of what, I cannot say, since a combination of delicacy and my respect for his memory forbid that I read further.

It's always a mistake to forget William of Occam and his razor. Look first for the simplest explanation that will handle the facts. I had always thought that perfectly normal human beings turned into bureaucrats and administrators and came to learn the language of that tribe through some exceedingly complicated combination of nature and nurture, through imitative osmosis and some flaw of character caused by inappropriate weaning. Piffle. These psychologists have captured our minds and led us into needless deviousness. The razor cuts to the heart of things and reveals the worm in the brain.

Admittedly, that may be a slight oversimplification. It may be that the decay of language and the desire to administrate are not merely concomitant symptoms of one and the same disease, but that *one* is a symptom and the other a symptom of the symptom. Let's imagine what deans, who like to imitate government functionaries, who, in their turn, like to imitate businessmen, who themselves seem to like to imitate show-business types, would call a "scenario."

There you sit, minding your own business and hurting no man. All at once, quite insensibly, the *thing* creeps into your brain. It might end up in the storage shelves of the subjunctive or the switchboard of the nonrestrictive clauses, of course, but in your case it heads for the cozy nook where the active and passive voices are balanced and adjusted. There it settles in and nibbles a bit here and a bit there. In our present state of knowledge, still dim, we have to guess that the active voice is tastier than the passive, since the destruction of the latter is very rare but of the former all too common.

So there you are with your active verbs being gnawed away. Little by little and only occasionally at first, you start saying things like: "I am told that . . ." and "This letter is being written because . . ." This habit has subtle effects. For one thing, since passives always require more words than actives, anything you may happen to write is longer than it would have been before the attack of the worm. You begin to suspect that you have a lot to say after all and that it's probably rather important. The suspicion is all the stronger because what you write has begun to sound — well, sort of "official." "Hmm," you say to yourself, "Fate may have cast my lot a bit below my proper station," or, more likely, "Hmm. My lot may have been cast by Fate a bit below my proper station."

Furthermore, the very way you consider the world, or the very way in which the world is considered by you, is subtly altered. You used to see a world in which birds ate worms and men made decisions. Now it looks more like a world in which worms are eaten by birds and decisions are made by men. It's almost a world in which victims are put forward as "doers" responsible for whatever may befall them and actions are almost unrelated to those who perform them. But only almost. The next step is not taken until you learn to see a world in which worms are eaten and decisions made and *all* responsible agency has disappeared. Now you are ready to be an administrator.

This is a condition necessary to successful administration of any sort and in any calling. Letters are written, reports are prepared, decisions made, actions taken, and consequences suffered. These things happen in the world where agents and doers, the responsible parties around whose throats we like our hands to be gotten, first retreat to the remoter portions of prepositional phrases and ultimately disappear entirely. A too-frequent use of the passive is not just a stylistic quirk; it is the outward and visible sign of a certain weltanschauung.

And now that it is *your* weltanschauung (remember the worm has been gnawing all this time), you discover that you are suited to the life of the administrator. You'll fit right in.

Therefore, we may say that it is not the worm in the skull that causes deans and managers and vice presidents, at least not directly. The worm merely causes the atrophy of the active and the compensatory dominance of the passive. (Through a similar compensatory mechanism, three-legged dogs manage to walk, and the language of the typical administrator is not very different from the gait of the three-legged dog, come to think of it.) The dominance of the passive causes in the victim an alteration of philosophy, which alteration is itself the thing that both beckons him to and suits him for the work of administration. And there you have it. Thanks to Carl Sagan and a little help from William of Occam, we understand how administrators come to be.

You may want to object that a whole view of the world and its meanings can hardly be importantly altered by a silly grammatical form. If so, you're just not thinking. Grammatical forms are *exactly* the things that make us understand the world the way we understand it. To understand the world, we make propositions about it, and those propositions are both formed and limited by the grammar of the language in which we propose.

To see how this works, let's imagine an extreme case. Suppose there *is* after all a place in the brain that controls the making and understanding of prepositional phrases. Suppose that Doctor Fu Manchu has let loose in the world the virus that eats that very place, so that in widening circles from Wimbledon mankind loses the power to make and understand prepositional phrases. Now the virus has gotten you, and to you prepositional phrases no longer make sense. You can't read them, you can't write them, you can't utter them, and when you hear them you can only ask "Wha?" Try it. Go read something, or look out the window and describe what you see. Tell the story of your day. Wait . . . you can't exactly do that . . . tell, instead, your day-story. Recite how you went working . . . how morning you went . . . no . . . morning not you . . . morning went . . . how you morning went . . . The rest will be silence.

Only through unspeakable exertion and even ad hoc invention of new grammatical arrangements can we get along at all without the prepositional phrase, as trivial as that little thing seems to be. It's more than that. Should we lose prepositional phrases, the loss of a certain arrangement of words would be only the visible sign of a stupendous unseen disorder. We would in fact have lost *prepositionalism*, so to speak, the whole concept of the kind of relationship that is signaled by the prepositional phrase. We'd probably be totally incapacitated.

Try now to imagine the history of mankind without the prepositional phrase, or, if you're tired of that, the relative clause or the distinction between subject and object. It would be absurd to think that lacking those and other such things the appearance and growth of human culture would have been merely hindered. It would have been impossible. *Everything* that we have done would have been simply impossible. The world out there is made of its own stuff, but the world that we can understand and manipulate and predict is made of discourse, and discourse is ruled by grammar. Without even so elementary a device as the prepositional phrase we'd be wandering around in herds right now, but we wouldn't know how to name what we were doing.

We're inclined to think of things like prepositional phrases as though they were optional extras in a language, something like whitewall tires. This is because we don't spend a lot of time dwelling on them except when we study a language not our own. We study German, and here comes a lesson on the prepositional phrase. Great, now we can *add* something to our German. That's the metaphor in our heads; we think — there *is* German, it exists, and when you get good at it you can add on the fancy stuff like prepositional phrases. All we have to do is memorize the prepositions and remember which ones take the dative and which ones take the accusative and which ones sometimes take the one and sometimes the other and when and why and which ones are the exceptions. Suddenly it becomes depressing. How about we forget the whole thing and settle for your stripped-down basic model German without any of the fancy stuff? If you do that, of course, you'll never find the *Bahnhof.* You'll be stymied in Stuttgart.

Like prepositional phrases, certain structural arrangements in English are much more important than the small bones of grammar in its most technical sense. It really wouldn't matter much if we started dropping the *s* from our plurals. Lots of words get along without it anyway, and in most cases context would be enough to indicate number. Even the distinction between singular and plural verb forms is just as much a polite convention as an essential element of meaning. But the structures, things like passives and prepositional phrases, constitute, among other things, an implicit system of moral philosophy, a view of the world *and* its presumed meanings, and their misuse therefore often betrays an attitude or value that the user might like to disavow.

Here's an example from the works of a lady who may also have a worm in her brain. She is "the chair" of the Equal Employment Opportunity Commission. It's very short and seems, to those willing to overlook a "small" grammatical flaw, almost too trivial to be worthy of comment. She writes: "Instead of accepting charges indiscriminately and giving them docket numbers, charging parties are counseled immediately."

"Charging parties" are probably faster than landing parties and larger than raiding parties, but no matter. She means, probably, people who are bringing charges of some sort, but there are many kinds of prose in which people become parties. It's not really meant to sound convivial, though: it's meant to sound "legal." What's important is that the structure of her sentence leads us to expect that the people (or parties) named first after that comma will also be the people (or parties) responsible for doing the "accepting." We expect something like: "Instead of doing *that*, we now do this." That's not because of some *rule*; it's just the way English works. It both reflects and generates the way the mind does its business in English. We, the readers, are disappointed and confused because somebody who ought to have shown up in this sentence has in fact not appeared. What has become of the *accepting* parties? Are they hanging around the water cooler? Do they refuse to accept? Are they at least hoping that no one will remember that they are *supposed* to accept? We can guess, of course, that they are the same people who make up the counseling parties, who have also disappeared into a little passive. It's as though we went charging down to the EEOC and found them all out to lunch.

Well, that could have been a slip of the mind, the mind of the chair, of course, but later we read: "Instead of dealing with charging parties and respondents through formalistic legal paper, the parties are called together within a few weeks..."

It's the same arrangement. Who does that dealing, or, since that's what they did before the "instead," who *did* that dealing through "formalistic" paper? Wouldn't they be the same parties who ought to do the calling together? Where have they all gone?

A schoolteacher would call those things examples of dangling modifiers and provide some rules about them, but that's not important. What's important is that those forms are evocations of that imagined world in which responsible agency is hardly ever visible, much to the comfort of responsible agency. Since that is the nature of the world already suggested by the passive voice, you would expect that this writer, or chair, would be addicted to the passive. You'd be right. Here are the bare skeletons of a few consecutive sentences:

... staff is assigned ...
... cases are moved ...
... parties are contacted ...
... files are grouped ... and prioritized ...

... steps are delineated ... and time frames established ...

... discussions are encouraged ...

You have to wonder how much of a discussion you could possibly have with these people. They're never around. Admittedly, it does these bureaucrats some credit that in their hearts they are ashamed to say that they actually do those things that they do. After all, who would want to tell the world that he, himself, in his very flesh, goes around grouping and prioritizing?

The dangling modifiers go well with the passives, and, in suggesting the nature of the world as seen by bureaucrats, they even add something new. The passives are sort of neutral, verbal shoulder-shrugs — these things happen — what can I tell you? The danglers go the next obvious and ominous step and suggest subtly that those charging parties have caused a heap of trouble and really ought to be handed the job of sorting things out for themselves, which, grammatically, is exactly what happens. In the first example the people who do the accepting and the counseling ought to appear right after the comma, but they don't. In the second, the people who do the dealing and the calling ought to appear right after the comma, but they don't. In both cases the people who *do* appear are the clients on whose behalf someone is supposed to accept, counsel, deal, and call. Does that mean something about the way in which those clients are regarded by this agency? They seem to have been put in some kind of grammatical double jeopardy, which is probably unconstitutional.

The poor lady, or chair, has inadvertently said what she probably meant. Working for the government would be so pleasant if it weren't for those pesky citizens. A waspish psychiatrist might observe that she has taken those charging parties and has "put them in their place" with a twist of grammar, thus unconsciously expressing her wish that they ought to be responsible for all the tedious labor their charges will cost her and her friends. She herself, along with the whole blooming EEOC, has withdrawn behind a curtain of cloudy English from the clash of charging parties on the darkling plain. "Ach so, sehr interessant, nicht wahr, zat ze patzient ist immer py ze Wort 'inshtead' gonvused. Es gibt, vielleicht, a broplem of, how you zay, Inshteadness." And indeed, the result of the dangling modifiers is to put the charging parties forth *instead* of someone else, as though the word had been chosen to stand out in front of the sentence as a symbol of the latent meaning.

Surely this lady, or chair, is an educated person, or chair, perfectly able to see and fix dangling modifiers of the sort they used to deal with in the early grades. After all, she has been hired as a chair, and for such a position we can assume some pretty high standards and stringent requirements. All right, so she doesn't know the difference between "formal" and "formalistic" — big deal. When such a high-ranking official of our government apparatus makes a mistake in structure, and habitually at that, it's not much to the point to underline it and put an exclamation mark in the margin. In a small child these would be mistakes; in a chair they are accidental revelations of a condition in the mind. To put the name of the thing modified as close as possible to the modifier is not a "rule" of English; it is a sign of something the mind does in English. When the English doesn't do that thing, it's because the mind hasn't done it.

It would be fatuous for us to say that we don't understand those sentences because of the disappearance of the people who are supposed to do all those things. It is a schoolteacher's cheap trick to say that if you don't get your grammar right people won't understand you. It's almost impossible to mangle grammar to that point where you won't be understood. We understand those sentences. In fact, we understand them better than the writer; we understand both what she thought she was saying and something else that she didn't think she was saying.

Many readers, of course, would "understand" those sentences without even thinking of the problem they present, and they might think these comments pedantic and contentious. Oh, come on, what's all the fuss? A couple of little mistakes. What does it matter? We all know what she means, don't we?

Such objections come from the erroneous idea that the point of language is merely to communicate, "to get your ideas across," whatever that means. Furthermore, such objectors may think that they are defending a hard-working and well-meaning chair, but she is little likely to be grateful for their partisanship if she figures out what it means. They say, in effect, that her little mistakes are just that, little mistakes rather than inadvertent and revealing slips of the mind. In the latter case, however, we can conclude that she is merely a typical bureaucrat with an appropriately managerial twist in the brain; in the former we would simply have to conclude that she is not well enough educated to be allowed to write public documents. Which of these conclusions do you suppose she would prefer? It seems that we must choose one or the other. Those are either mistakes made in ignorance or mistakes made in something other than ignorance.

The mind, thinking in English, does indubitably push modifiers and things modified as close together as possible. Can there really be a place in the brain where that happens, a function that might be damaged or dulled? It doesn't matter, of course, because there is surely a "place" in the mind analogous to the imagined place in the brain.

Whether by worms or world-views, it does seem sometimes to be invaded and eaten away. The malfunctions we can see in this chair and in my erstwhile friend, now an assistant dean pro tem, are small inklings of a whole galaxy of disorders that has coalesced out of the complicated history of language, of our language in particular, and out of the political history of language in general.

# 2

# The
# Two Tribes

The Jiukiukwe Indians live in some swamps near the
headwaters of the Orinoco. They are the most primitive
people on the face of the earth, and their homeland is so
isolated and dismal and totally lacking in anything of
value that they will never be discovered by civilized men.

They do not know the use of fire. They wear no cloth-
ing, although on special occasions the married men do
drape pieces of vines around their necks. They don't tie
them, however, for they have not discovered the knot.
They build no shelters, and they use no tools, except for
unworked rocks with which they bang on trees in order
to dislodge the bark and expose the grubs and worms on
which they live. Once in a while they find a dead fish
floating in the water close enough to the shore to be
hauled in without having to wade out too far. The waters
teem with nasty creatures. They celebrate the occasion
with a communal meal and a religious festival, at the

climax of which the married men drape the pieces of vine around their necks. When the party is over, they squat happily in the muck and jabber away at each other in a language that contains thirty-four separate noun declensions, each providing forty-five separate forms, fifteen singulars, fifteen duals, and fifteen plurals.

Their verbs are even more complicated. The conjugations, eleven in all, indicate not only the usual things like person, number, tense, voice, and mood, but also the relationship of the speaker to his listener. A younger brother who is nevertheless not the youngest of his mother's sons and who has never found a fish must speak, in the dry season, to the eldest of his paternal uncles in verb forms that would scandalize the mother-in-law of his youngest female cousin, especially in the rainy season.

The Jiukiukwe language has an enormous vocabulary in matters of interest to the Jiukiukwe. Although their technology is limited to the banging of trees with stones, they have scores of words to describe it. They have separate and unrelated words for flat stones, round stones, big stones, little stones, sharp stones, and so on, but they have no word for "stone." In the case of trees, the vocabulary is even larger, since trees in which grubs or worms have been found are distinguished individually from one another by words that amount almost to "names" and are devised as needed, while unproductive trees or trees not yet banged are named not for any physical attributes but for their location with reference to the nearest tree that has provided grubs and worms. The whole system is duplicated with utterly unrelated words for fallen trees. They have, however, no word that simply means "tree."

Since they use their knuckles and fingertips for counting, they can count only up to thirty-eight. (They count three knuckles on each finger but only two on the thumb.)

Counting begins with the knuckle at the base of the left little finger, moves out to the tip, continues starting with the knuckle at the base of the ring finger, and so forth. Each hand thus provides nineteen units. Every knuckle and every fingertip has its own name, and those names are also the names of the numbers. They have, however, no names for the toes, and, while they do speak of the arms and the legs, they use one and the same word to name the ankles, knees, wrists, and elbows.

"Correct" social behavior among the Jiukiukwe is entirely a matter of doing and saying the right thing to the right relative under the right circumstances. Accordingly, the vocabulary and grammar of kinship are very large and complex. They have separate words for every possible degree of familial relationship. Not only, for instance, is there a special word for the oldest son of your mother's next youngest sister, but there is yet another word for him should he have reached that estate through the death of some older brother. In either case, he is called by still another name until sunset on a day when he has found a dead fish. However, since all the Jiukiukwe are related to one another in some precisely nameable way, they have no need for words that mean things like "family" or "relative" or "kinship."

There is a curious thing about the way they use their verbs. They have, of course, both passive and active forms, but they consider it a serious breach of etiquette amounting almost to sacrilege to use the active form when speaking of persons. In a child, the use of the active voice in the first person singular is taken somewhat less seriously, but it is still discouraged as a mark of arrogance or aggressiveness. Indeed, their words for "angry" and "insane" both contain an element of the ending that goes with the first person singular in that conjugation most often used by young children. They do not say: "I am eating my worm." They say rather: "With regard to the worm unto me, there is an occasion of eating." Animals and objects, however, are normally found as subjects of active verbs. The sun rises and the worm crawls, subject only to those forms available to that person who is saying those things and to whom he says them.

Their language sounds terribly complicated, and it is. It is every bit as complicated as English, or any other language, for that matter. All languages are complicated beyond hope of complete description. When it seems to us that German is less difficult to learn than Arabic, what we have noticed is not that German is less complicated than Arabic but that German is the more like English. Speaking his language is the most complicated thing a human being does, and should he undertake to go even further and learn to read and write it, he multiplies one infinitude of complications by another. It is an awesome marvel that anyone can do any of these things, never mind do them well.

Nevertheless, billions of people speak and understand a language. In fact, unless there's something wrong, every human being there is speaks and understands at least one language. Every member of *Homo sapiens* ever born spoke and understood a language, unless, of course, he died too soon or was in some special way disabled. The ability to use language is included in the meaning of *sapiens*. We have no other way of being *sapiens* except through language. The Jiukiukwe may lack barbecue pits and some of our other things, but they are every bit as *sapiens* as the inhabitants of Manhasset. They have all it takes.

Still, they are different from the inhabitants of Manhasset in many ways. The material differences come easily to mind, since the Manhassetites have not only barbecue pits but much more, but there is a much more important difference than that. It is this: In the same circumstance, the Manhassetite will say, "I want food" and the Jiukiukwe will say, "As for me, there is hunger." Every other difference is because of this difference; this is *the* difference between the Manhassetites and the Jiukiukwe, the difference from which all smaller differences flow.

The Manhassetites speak a language in which the typical statement takes the form of a sentence that names a doer and his deed. The most common elaboration also names the "object" of his deed. "I want food" displays exactly the typical structure of the most ordinary Manhassetite utterance. The structure may be modified and elaborated in many ways, some of them quite extensive and complicated, but it remains the enduring skeleton of the typical statement: A doer does something, often *to* something or someone. The continuous reappearance of this structure has taught all Manhassetites a particular view of the world and man's place in it. They understand the world as a place where doers do things. That is why many of them will get raises next year and dig bigger barbecue pits.

The Jiukiukwe, on the other hand, have been taught by the basic structure of their language that *doing* is properly the business of the things in the world around them. Nor do they think of themselves, again because of their grammar, as the "objects" of the things that are done in the world. For the Jiukiukwe, the inanimate or animal doers of deeds do them at most "insofar as he is concerned," as though he were, if not always an unaffected bystander, at least no more than accidentally related to what happens in the world. The Jiukiukwe are just *there*; the world does its things around them, sometimes "in their case."

They will not get any raises next year, and you can easily see why they have no barbecue pits to enlarge. Technological change comes about when somebody does things to something. The Jiukiukwe have always lived, and will always live, exactly as they do today. Their technology will not change unless the basic structure of their language changes, although it may also be possible that the basic structure of their language would change should their technology change. There's no way of knowing which must come first, if either, but it seems more likely that the language must change before the technology unless some imported technology should come along and eventually force a change in the language.

Imagine that some particularly eccentric or mildly demented Jiukiukwe should develop the rude habit of speaking in the active and saying things like "I will find worms." He has now announced, to the Jiukiukwe way of thinking, some purported fact about the world and has at the same time subjected himself to considerable social disapproval. If he's to get back into the good graces of his older sister's father-in-law, and of everybody else, he had damn well better come up with the worms. The more the better. Then his arrogant statement might be re-understood and perhaps accepted indeed as a statement of fact about the world. In desperation, he might well discover that you can find more worms by prying off the bark with a sharp-edged stone than by banging the tree till the bark falls off. It might occur to him that some sharp stones are easier to hold and manipulate than others. Remember, he's going to work hard; they're all waiting for him to find worms and thus justify a statement in which he spoke of himself as one might speak of the sun or the moon. That's serious. It won't be long before he finds an obviously broken stone that works very well, and then it will come to him that he might bang some of those less efficient round stones together until *they* break and turn into good worm-diggers. Out of the active voice, a technology will be born. Before long, his relatives, noticing how plump and healthy he looks, will learn to copy both his magics, his verbs as well as his stones, and that will be the end of civilization as the Jiukiukwe know it.

When a Manhassetite faces a problem, he asks, drawing upon the basic structure of his language, "What shall I do?" He looks for an action to perform. The Jiukiukwe is unlikely even to think that he faces a problem, since that itself is a case of an agent doing something to something. Significantly, the Jiukiukwe language has no word for "problem." "Problem" can be thought of only in a language that can also think of "solution," and the relationship between the two is understood through a grammar that permits the idea of doers doing things. The Jiukiukwe do not think of a shortage of worms as a "problem," a condition whose very name suggests that somebody might do something about something. They think of it as a "badness," "a state of few worms in relation to us," a condition in the world that just happens to affect them.

Although the Jiukiukwe seem to pay a heavy price for their grammar, they also take from it some advantages not available to the Manhassetites. They have, for instance, no warfare, because warfare not only arises from the willed deeds of agents but is itself a matter of willing agents doing things to each other. In any case, they don't even have the individual analogues of war: hatred, envy, and competitiveness. The Manhassetites are a small subgroup of a large, warlike tribe, which is, in turn, only one of many tribes loosely associated into an enormous culture in which warfare is a permanent institution and even the root of much of its most vigorous enterprise. Naturally, hatred, envy, and competition are almost universal among individual Manhassetites. For the Jiukiukwe there is essentially only one doer of things, and that is something like the world itself, which does what it does neither out of will nor out of design. It has no intentions; it just happens. For the Manhassetites, there are as many possible doers as there are members of the species or nouns in the language, and their grammar encourages them to envision a universe in which conflict of intentions is simply a part of the fabric of reality.

An idea of reality is what we devise and perceive through our language; reality itself is probably something else again. Both the Jiukiukwe and the Manhassetites fancy that they know the real world, but what they know is some presumed order of things symbolized and suggested by the vocabularies and structures of their languages. They live by grammar; all men do. That's why the grammars of all languages are so terribly complicated. There are no people, however "primitive," who see the world as a simple place. In fact, the more "primitive" they are, the more complicated and elaborate the assumed underlying structure of reality in their languages. Furthermore, there seem to be no people who are content to have a language in which to consider only the world of sensible experience, and all languages are anchored mostly in other worlds rather than the one that we experience here and now.

It's fun, and safe, to speculate on the origins of language. What makes it fun is obvious, but what makes it safe is that no dreary scholar will ever come along with the facts to prove what a fool you've been. If you speculate on Milton's toilet-training or the social structures of the leaf-cutting ants, the very next mail will bring you a fat journal containing the definitive findings. The mystery of the origin of language is the linguist's equivalent of the physicist's mystery of the nature of the universe, if any, before the big bang. The evidence we need is utterly inaccessible, and there's no way to draw valid conclusions from the evidence we have. Even experimentation is impossible. The story has been told, for instance, of several famous despots, that they had some newborn children raised from infancy by deaf-mute nursemaids to see what language they would speak. It turned out that children thus raised do not, after all, grow up speaking Hebrew, the supposed language of God and the angels. They grow up, of course, speaking nothing. Learning your language seems not at all analogous to developing one. Such an experiment would tell us nothing about the origin of language even if we could keep it going for thousands of years and watch generation after generation. The brains and even the vocal apparatus of those in whom language began were significantly different from ours, and our isolated infants would begin with an *evolved* propensity for language. It would surely be an interesting experiment, but it would tell us nothing about *the* origin of language.

It is just as much fun, however, and somewhat more useful to speculate about something that was probably *not* the origin of language, although we sometimes carelessly think that it might have been. There is a kind of everyday, commonsense notion about the origin of language that sticks in our heads and causes important misunderstandings. It is, of course, the notion that language must have begun as a way of naming things in the world in which we live. Those are exactly the things that need no naming.

The world in which we live is very tiny; it is as tiny for the Manhassetites as it is for the Jiukiukwe. That world can only be the world of immediate sensory experience, the world we can perceive in whatever way we can in this moment, which is now gone. The world of sensory experience is so tiny and so brief that, in a sense, we can't *do* anything in it; we can only *be* in it. The world that *was* before this moment is immeasurably big, and so too the world that will be, to say nothing of the world that might have been or the world that may yet be or, the root of morality, the world that someone thinks *should* be. It is the main business of language to evoke such worlds.

The speechless animals live entirely in the world that is. It is sometimes said that some of the animals have a "language" with which they send signals to one another about the world that is. That's nonsense. That we can uncritically accept such nonsense is testimony to the power of grammar. "Animals send signals" is a satisfying appearance of the basic structure of our language, and it harmonizes sweetly with our concomitant idea that the world is a place where most of what happens can be understood as the act of an agent who is doing something. The animals are not agents committing acts. When a zebra out on the edge of the herd sniffs a lion in the tall grass, he does not say to himself in any fashion, "I had better tell the others." (Nor would you, for that matter.) He simply does what is appropriate for a successful zebra to do under those circumstances. His startled neighbors, startled by what he does whether they sniff lion or not, do likewise. That's part of how they got to be grown-up zebras in the first place. The zebras who are slow to startle have a way of dropping out of the herd early in life. In a moment, the whole herd is in flight, but it cannot be properly said that a zebra has sent a message. It would be more accurate to say that the zebras have caught something from one another.

Human beings, too, catch things from one another, and usually with no use of language at all. We can imagine the hominid and speechless precursors of man wandering not far from the zebras. What need could they possibly have had to call the lion by a name? Just as surely as the zebras, they must have reacted appropriately to a whiff of lion. If they hadn't, they wouldn't have been around long enough to provide a future for all of us. What need, for that matter, would they have had to name the food they were eating or seeking, the food of the world of experience? Would they have had to be "told" to feed the young? To sleep at night? No animals need names for such things, because they do not have to "tell" of them. Such things, in their seasons, are just *there*. Language is for telling, not for naming. Nobody needs to be told that he is getting wet in the rain or that he is eating a banana.

Think what happens when you encounter an unexpected snake, the usual kind. There is no word in your head, no language at all, in the instant of automatic recoil. *Then* you say, if only in your head, "Oh, a snake." The word "snake" makes you feel better, because it opens the gates for many other words. It occurs to you, because you have the words *in which* it occurs to you, that most snakes found in Manhasset are harmless and unaggressive and that you're not really in danger. You have transformed a creature in the world of sense experience into a whole system of related ideas in a world that is not the world of sense experience. That little chill was real, and, for a moment, it remains, but you are not in flight. You are in another world, the world where snakes are made of discourse, not blood and bones and teeth. Your language gives you access to that world.

The Jiukiukwe are also afraid of snakes, and they have better reasons than we. The swamps are full of them, and none of them is harmless. Members of the tribe sometimes die of snakebite, and little children out looking for dead fish have occasionally been swallowed by anacondas. In the company of an anaconda, any forest animal is afraid, just like any Jiukiukwe. The difference, though, is that the Jiukiukwe have a language so that they don't have to wait to be afraid until they actually find themselves in the company of the anaconda. They can be afraid ahead of time. In language they remember the anaconda of the past and take thought for the anaconda of the future. *Those* big snakes are not around to inspire fear; they are in other worlds. Language evokes them.

The Jiukiukwe use a part of the word for anaconda to describe those places where the snakes have been seen in the past. With the appropriate verb ending, of course, the same word is used to shoo children away from things. This is actually a form of technology, or, at least, social engineering, since it makes the children anxious and more than ordinarily observant when they are in places that carry that name. In spite of the obvious fact that there aren't *always* anacondas to be found in those places, the language behaves as though there were. Some world other than the world of experience is projected by the use of an adjective. When we can project such an alternative world, we can also find, sometimes, a way of bringing it home and thus changing the world of immediate experience.

In language, man can project a world in which he doesn't get soaked by every rain that falls. In that language, he can also reconstruct some past world in which he found himself under an overhanging cliff that kept him out of the rain. He can start looking for cliffs. He can eventually project a world in which some artificial cliff keeps him out of the rain and provides him with a quiet, comfortable afternoon in which to refine the invention of architecture. Such projections require language, not merely the naming of things.

People who have merely come up with a word for "wet" can do nothing more than stand around in the rain announcing to each other a sorry fact that needs no announcing. It won't help them, either, to come up with a word for "dry." What they need is a way to think about "dry" even while they are getting wet, a way to relate the two even when only one is present in the world of experience. They need "wet could be dry." That's grammar.

A collection of names for things in the world, however large, does not make a language. A language is only incidentally in the business of naming things. Its important business is to explore the way in which things are, or perhaps might be, related to one another. Building a shelter takes more than words for "dry" and "cliff." It needs an idea of relationship, the idea of "under." Then it needs another relationship, one that might be understood by something like "dry under *made* cliff." To that, some designing mind must add not only "tomorrow" but "all tomorrows." "Cliff" names something in the palpable world, and "dry" names not exactly a thing in the world but at least a physical condition. Those other words, however, "made" and "tomorrow" and "all," name nothing in this world. They name some ways in which things can be related to each other.

How such words came to be is a profound mystery, every bit as vexatious as the mystery surrounding the birth of language itself. Perhaps, even probably, they are the same mystery, for there certainly could be no such thing as language without them. The ability to discern and name the relationships suggested, for instance, by words like "so" and "if" was more important to the history of man than fire or the wheel, neither of which would have been ours without "so" and "if."

Even many of the words that we think of as the names of things in the world are really descriptions of relationships that exist only in the world of language. The Jiukiukwe, remember, have no word for "stone," since for them stones *as* stones have no interest. To them, what we would call a pile of stones is a pile of tree-bangers, a name not intended to point at the things themselves but to their place in the life of the Jiukiukwe. To some other crowd of savages the same pile of stones might well be a pile of "weapons." Stones are indeed found lying around on the ground, but weapons and tree-bangers are found in systems of culture.

Similarly, when the Jiukiukwe have a word for every possible family relationship, it's not because they are naming precisely this or that person who actually exists before their very eyes. They are naming *places* in a complicated social design, not people. The social system exists in their minds, but it can exist there only because the language sets it forth for the mind to understand. They would say that *we* are primitive in our appreciation of family life because we can name so few relationships, just as we say that they are primitive because they use the same word for "knee" and "elbow." From their point of view, we are just that backward because we call all the sons of our mothers by the one word "brother."

People who can remember only one line of Wittgenstein are likely to remember his terse suggestion that we ought to keep our mouths shut about matters whereof we can tell nothing. This dictum provides some interesting corollaries. One of them is that in matters where we *do* keep our mouths shut, we can have no knowledge. If, for instance, there should exist something that a language has no way of expressing, then that thing does not "exist" for the culture that speaks the language. For all their compulsive attention to their relatives, the Jiukiukwe, as you know, have no word for "family." They are all related. Since we are not, we need the word "family" as a term of distinction. In like fashion, every word isolates the thing named from everything else that there is, whether it be the name of some object in the world of experience or some idea of relationship in the world of language. In effect, everything that gets a name gets it because we can perceive that everything else is *not* that thing. Even the simple abstraction "stones," therefore, is for us just as much a recognition of a relationship as "tree-bangers" is for the Jiukiukwe. The relationship of "stones" to everything that is not "stones" we can perceive. Of those relationships that we do not, for one reason or another, perceive, we cannot speak, and thus we can have no knowledge.

Our knowledge is made up of the stories that we can tell, stories that must be told in the language that we know. (Even mathematics is a "language" that states propositions and tells stories. It's a very elaborate form of "play" language. That's why it's such fun for those who speak it well.) Where we can tell no story, we can have no knowledge. That's probably why we all have amnesia about infancy. As infants, we hadn't the language with which to transform the world of experience into the more durable form of knowledge and memory. When our forebears had no language and no knowledge, the best they could do was sniff the lion in the long grass. That wasn't too bad, of course, and thousands of other kinds of creatures have done quite well with nothing more. But when we found language and became *Homo sapiens* (how could those events have been anything other than simultaneous?), we could tell ourselves the story of the last time we passed this way and lost Gbloog to a lion. Even more important, we could invent the story of the *next* time and either be prepared for a lion or decide to take the long way around. To deal with the lion here and now, we don't need language, just a good nose and strong legs. Language can deal with the lion that was and the lion that will be, even the lion that *may* be. Creatures who can speak can survive even if they have bad noses and short, stumpy legs.

In those times, linguistic ability must have brought an even better hope of survival than physical prowess. The silly boob who just couldn't get into his head the implications of the future conditional, accordingly, was just a hair more likely to be eaten by lions than his lame but more intellectual brother. A new element had appeared in the process of natural selection. Nowadays, we notice that there is very little danger of being eaten by lions. Nevertheless, the destiny that waits in the long grass for the silly boob who can't get his language straight is not a good one, although, of course, it does last longer than the business of being eaten by a lion. It's more like being eaten by a worm, slowly.

# 3

# A Bunch
# of Marks

Still, skill in language does provide a better hope of survival; it even wins wars, for struggle on the field of battle
is a dramatic version of strife in the minds of men. Long
before the first trigger was pulled, Hitler fired off a shat-
tering salvo of words. He pounded his fist and shouted:
*"Ein Volk, ein Reich, ein Führer!"* Don't make the mistake of thinking that his listeners muttered back an uncertain *"Ach so, gewiss, gewiss."* They shouted back,
*"Ein Volk, ein Reich, ein Führer!"*

The cannonade roared across the Channel and shook
the cliffs of England. Fortunately for us all, England,
although unarmed, was not unready. The answering bar-
rage rings in our ears still: "Blood, toil, tears, and sweat."
Battle was joined. Hitler's words sent the Wehrmacht
crashing to the outskirts of Dunkirk, but Churchill's
words sent schoolboys and accountants and retired fish-
mongers down to the sea in their little boats and over the
water to the beaches of Dunkirk.

While that may be an incomplete account of the war, it is not an inaccurate one. It was a war of words and speaking just as much as a war of iron and blood. If the fighting was sometimes noble and brave, it was because certain words were in the minds of men. If the fighting was sometimes stupid and vicious, it was because certain other words were in the minds of men. Whatever else Churchill may have been doing in those days, he was always providing the English with words. With words he formed their thoughts and emotions. "We shall fight on the beaches, we shall fight on the landing grounds, we shall fight in the fields and in the streets, we shall fight in the hills," said Churchill. Millions answered, apparently, "By God, so we shall."

Imagine, however, that Churchill had been an ordinary bureaucrat and had chosen to say instead:

> Consolidated defensive positions and essential pre-planned withdrawal facilities are to be provided in order to facilitate maximum potentialization for the repulsion and/or delay of incursive combatants in each of several preidentified categories of location deemed suitable to the emplacement and/or debarkation of hostile military contingents.

That would, at least, have spared us the pain of wondering what to do about the growing multitudes who can't seem to read and write English. By now we'd be wondering what to do about the growing multitudes who can't seem to read and write German.

Speech is tremendously powerful. It moves our minds and makes the path of history. It is, furthermore, perhaps the most complicated skill we have, and the uttering of words and sentences is only its beginning. When we speak, we do many other things simultaneously. We turn our heads and lift our eyebrows and wiggle our fingers and get up and walk about. We find exactly the right place from which to say *this* thing, and we go over to lean on the mantelpiece to say some other thing. We choose the appropriate pitch and volume for every sound. We sprinkle our speech with nonverbal sound effects, snorts and mm's, sighs and tsk's, and especially pauses, which are as important to speech as the rests to music. We change the shapes of our mouths and throats and alter the very tone quality of our voices. All such things, and innumerably more, we do quite automatically, and with such devices we suggest immeasurably more than the words can say by themselves.

Writing, on the other hand, is just a bunch of marks. It is *not* speech written down, and it lacks almost all the expressive devices of speech. It simply isn't "natural" in the way that speech is natural. For the natural expressive devices of speech, writing provides only a few pathetically inadequate gimmicks. We have some marks of punctuation and some graphic tricks, like capital letters and underlining. We can find an occasional word or expression that may remind a reader of the sound of speech, you know, and drop it in here and there. An occasional genius learns to write dialogue that we can almost hear and even to devise long passages that *sound* exactly right, but in general writing is even further from speech than notation is from music.

Like music, speech has a tune, and we have only the meagerest ways of indicating on the page the tune to which our words are to be sung. Commas, for instance, are pretty good as indicators of tune, and so are periods. They usually call for bits of melody that every native speaker of English sings in pretty much the same way. Question marks, however, indicate only a certain "family" of tunes, for any question we can make in English can be sung in many different ways to convey many different meanings. All these gimmicks, nevertheless, even the quotation marks that suggested a certain way to sing "family" in the last sentence, can't come close to a realistic approximation of the tune of English. And even if they could, they still wouldn't tell you which word was to be said slowly and deep in the throat and what sentence was to be delivered while leaning on the mantelpiece. As a way of recording speech, writing is a dismal failure.

It doesn't matter, though, because the recording of speech is not the proper business of writing. The proper business of writing is to stay put on the page so that we can look at it later. Writing, whether it be a grocery list or *The Brothers Karamazov*, freezes the work of the mind into a permanent and public form. It is the mind and memory of mankind in such a form that we can pass it around to one another and even hand it on to our unimaginably remote descendants.

Language is, essentially, speech. Writing is a special case of language. Discursive prose is a special case of writing. Written, discursive prose may be almost three thousand years old, but it is still our most recently invented use of language. It is no coincidence that the Greeks who first devised discursive prose also constructed formal logic and were the first to provide for *their* unimaginably remote descendants a visible record of the works of their minds. Thinking *is* coherent discourse, and the logic and the prose require one another.

The mind is a rudderless wanderer blown here or there by any puff of breeze. If I mention watermelons, you must think of watermelons; if giraffes, giraffes. The very rare genius can keep his mind on course for a while, perhaps as long as a whole minute, but most of us are always at the mercy of every random suggestion of environment. We imagine that we sit down and think, but, in fact, we mostly gather wool, remembering this and that and fantasizing about the other. In our heads we recite some slogans and rehash the past, often repeatedly. Even in this foolish maundering, we are easily distracted by random thoughts, mostly about money or politics but often about sports or sex. Left to its own devices, the mind plays like a child in a well-stocked sandbox, toying idly with trinkets and baubles and often doing the same thing over and over again until some slightly more interesting game presents itself.

If we want to pursue extended logical thought, thought that can discover relationships and consequences and devise its own alternatives, we need a discipline imposed from outside of the mind itself. Writing is that discipline. It seems drastic, but we have to suspect that coherent, continuous thought is impossible for those who cannot construct coherent, continuous prose.

"Writing," Bacon said, "maketh an exact man," as we all know, but we ordinarily stop thinking about that too soon. The "exact" part is only half of what writing makes; the other half is the "man." Writing does indeed make us exact, because it leaves a trail of thought that we can retrace and so discover where we have been stupid. At the same time, though, it makes us "men," grown-ups who can choose what toys we want to play with and who can outwit the random suggestions of environment. In his writing, then, we can judge of at least two things in a man — his ability to think and his intention to do so, his maturity. An education that does not teach clear, coherent writing cannot provide our world with thoughtful adults; it gives us instead, at the best, clever children of all ages.

To understand the importance of writing for people who want to have a civilization, it is useful to compare discursive prose with poetry. Poetry is much older than prose, but since we have been taught to think it a form of "art," we regularly assume that prose comes first and that poetry, a much trickier business, is "refined" out of it with pain and skill. Not so. Many of the qualities that make poetry what it is are far more "natural" to any speaker of a language than the devices of prose. Like speech, poetry is metaphorical and figurative, elliptical, often more expressive than informative, synthetic rather than analytic, and concrete rather than abstract. Speech may not often be *good* poetry, whatever that may be, but sometimes it *is*. Little children devise poetic expressions quite naturally, and there seems to be no culture, however "primitive" we may think it, without its traditional poetry. Even the wretched Jiukiukwe have poetry.

The Jiukiukwe, like all other human beings, have some practical uses for poetry. In little verses, they can remember without effort the signs of a coming storm and the looks of the worms that cause diarrhea, just as we remember how many days there are in April. In poetry, or in language that is like poetry, they perform the social rituals that hold them together. That's exactly what we do when we recite the traditional formulae of recognition: Good to see you; What's new?; Lovely weather we're having. All such forms are permissible variations within the limits of established rituals that we all perform just because we're here and we're all in this together. We can remember and recite those ritual greetings just as easily as we can sing Fa-la-la-la-la and come in on the chorus — all together now!

(Digression: Why do we devote so much idle talk to the weather? Everybody knows, of course, that the weather is a "safe" subject, but that doesn't answer the question. It provides two new questions: *Why* is the weather a safe subject? and, Why do we devote so much idle talk to safe subjects?

The weather is right *there* in the world of experience. Even assistant deans pro tem can see that it's raining. When I meet the assistant dean pro tem on the campus in the rain, I am likely to assert, in one way or another, that it *is* in fact raining. He is likely to confirm this observation, after his fashion. We have used language where no language is needed, to indicate what *is* in the world of experience. To point out the rain to each other seems about as useful as mentioning the fact that we are both walking on our hind legs. That may be exactly why it's useful. We have taken the trouble to name something that needs no naming, thus acknowledging our kinship while still being careful not to evoke some other world in which our kinship might be questionable. Should I greet the assistant dean pro tem by announcing that power corrupts, he may well reply, "Absolutely!" and we will have evoked some other world, a world we'd rather not explore just now with the rain dripping down the backs of our necks. Twain probably had the truth in mind when he said that everyone talks about the weather but that nobody *does* anything about it. In fact, we talk about it precisely *because* we can't do anything about it. It permits us to establish our membership, which is polite, but it doesn't require that we look at each other's credentials too closely, which might be rude.)

Poetry is a profoundly conservative use of language. It conserves not only values and ideas but the very language itself, so that even some grammatical forms that ought to have disappeared long ago are still around and useful for special effects. Even crackpots who want to simplify and modernize English cannot bring themselves to say: Thirty days has September. It's amazing, but that actually *sounds wrong*, almost as wrong as: Six days shall you labor.

Prose is progressive and disruptive. It must subvert or elude the poetic qualities of speech to go about the business of logic and analysis. Discursive prose is essentially antisocial, subject to constraints and regulations that would be unsuitable, perhaps even rude, in speech. Writing is an audacious and insolent act. When we write, we call the other members of our tribe to order. We command their attention. We assert that what we have to say is valuable enough that they should give over their idle chitchat about the weather. It had better be.

When we choose to address our friends and relatives in discursive prose, it must be because what we want to say requires the special powers of discursive prose: logic, order, and coherence. The mere appearance of discursive prose promises those things. When I meet the assistant dean pro tem in the rain, I send and expect signals of fellowship. When I read his latest guidelines for the work of the Committee on Memorial Plaques, I hold in my hands a promise of logic, order, and coherence, and equally a promise that the language I read will be constrained and regulated in such a way as to engender those things. There is no Rule in Heaven that language has to be logical, orderly, and coherent any more than there is some Law of Nature that requires football players to stay within the lines. You can grab a football and run to Oshkosh anytime you please; you just won't be playing football. Your language can be illogical, disorderly, and even incomprehensible — in fact, sometimes it *should* be so — but you won't be writing discursive prose.

Ordinary speech, like poetry, is a kind of art; discursive prose in particular, like writing in general, is a technology.

Clear, concise writing is a result of good technique, like an engine that starts and runs.

Good technique requires the knowledge and control of many conventional forms and devices. They must be conventional because writing is public and enduring, and the path of its thought must be visible to other minds in other times. Like the conventional "rules" of any technology, the rules of writing have come to be what they are because they work. You do well to keep the subject of your sentence clearly in view just as you do well to keep your powder dry and your eye on the ball. These things work.

Furthermore, although such things are matters of technique, they are derived not from some concern for technique but because they go to the heart of *the* matter. You keep your eye on the ball because it *is* the ball, and the meaning of the game is known only because of what happens to the ball. You get no points for cute panties. You keep your eye on the subject because it *is* the subject, and not just grammatically. It is the subject of thought, and the sentence is a proposition about it. We do not think by naming things but by making propositions about them. Nor do we think by making propositions about unnamed or unnameable things. Any writer forgets that from time to time, but a learned rule of technology calls him to order. The rules of the technology of discursive prose are simply aids to thought, and to learn the conventions of writing without learning the habit of thought is impossible.

Fools and scoundrels say that the time of writing is past, that Direct Distance Dialing and the cassette recorder have done to writing what the internal combustion engine did to the art of equitation. They point out, quite correctly by the way, that the ordinary American, once released from the schools, can go through all the rest of his life without ever having to devise a complete sentence. Even the thousands of forms we have to fill out call only for filling in blanks or checking boxes. This freedom from writing, in fact, doesn't always have to wait on our escape from the schools; fewer and fewer schools require any of it at all. This is, they tell us, an age of technology, and that what we need to know is how to program computers, not how to devise grammatical sentences in orderly sequence.

As it happens, computers work by reading and devising grammatical sentences in orderly sequence. The "language" is different, but that's how they work. Their "rules" are far more stringent and unforgiving than the rules of discursive prose. When we read a sentence whose subject and verb don't agree, we don't reject it as meaningless and useless. We may shake our heads and sigh a little, but we know what the poor fellow meant, and we go on. When the computer "reads" a "sentence" with an equivalent error, it simply spits it out and refuses to work. That's how we can tell which are the machines and which the people; the people will swallow anything. And *you* will swallow anything if you believe that we can teach all that computer stuff to whole herds of people who haven't been able to master the elementary logic of subject-verb agreement.

The logic of writing is simply logic; it is not some system of arbitrary conventions interesting only to those who write a lot. All logical thought goes on in the form of statements and statements about statements. We can make those statements only in language, even if that language be a different symbol system like mathematics. If we cannot make those statements and statements about statements logically, clearly, and coherently, then we cannot think and make knowledge. People who cannot put strings of sentences together in good order cannot think. An educational system that does not teach the technology of writing is preventing thought.

# 4

# The Voice
# of Sisera

The invention of discursive prose liberated the mind of
man from the limitations of the individual's memory.
We can now "know" not just what we can store in our
heads, and, as often as not, misplace among the memora-
bilia and used slogans. Nevertheless, that invention made
concrete and permanent one of the less attractive facts
of language. It called forth a new "mode" of language
and provided yet another way in which to distinguish
social classes from one another.

Fleeing the lost battle on the plain of Megiddo, General Sisera is said to have stopped off at the tent of Heber
the Kenite. Heber himself was out, but his wife, Jael, was
home and happy to offer the sweaty warrior a refreshing
drink — "a bottle of milk" in fact, the Bible says. (That
seems to find something in translation.) It was a kindly
and generous gesture, especially since Sisera asked nothing more than a drink of water.

Having drunk his fill, the tired Sisera stretched out for a little nap and told Jael to keep careful watch, for he had good reason to expect that the Jews who had cut up his army that day were probably looking around for him. Jael said, Sure, sure, don't worry, and when Sisera fell asleep, that crafty lady took a hammer and a tent spike and nailed him through the temples fast to the earth.

I suppose that we are meant to conclude that the Kenites, not themselves Jews, were nevertheless right-thinking folk and that Jael's act had a meaning that was both political and religious. I'm not so sure. I'd like to know, before deciding, just what language it was that Sisera used when he asked for that drink of water.

Scholars think that Sisera was probably the leader of an invading Hittite army, but the details are not important. What is important is that he was obviously a would-be conqueror in a land not his own. He had, until quite recently, been successful; he had come a long way with his iron chariots, powerful weapons that the Jews lacked and that would have won yet another battle if it hadn't been for a spell of bad weather. He was a successful foreign invader from a technologically superior culture. Can you suppose that he felt any obligation or even curious desire to learn the language of the Jews? Wouldn't they have seemed to him just another bunch of local primitives, in no important way to be distinguished from other such bunches he had already overcome? As for the tent-dwelling Kenites, a meager clan of impoverished nomads, who would ever bother to learn their ignorant babble? I'm willing to bet a brand-new Fowler against a D minus freshman theme that Sisera spoke to Jael in his language, not hers, and loudly. With gestures. What Jael did, a little later, was actually an early example of linguistic consciousness-raising. Hers, not his.

Now, your typical American tourist in Naples doesn't usually get a wooden spike through his head for shouting pidgin English at the natives — a little diarrhea, maybe, but that's about it. Roman legionnaires in Gaul, however, and British soldiers in India did get some of each, once in a while. Conquered peoples hate, along with everything else about them, the language of the conquerors, and with good reason, for the language is itself a weapon. It keeps the vanquished in the dark about meanings and intentions, and it makes it extremely difficult to obey commands that had damn well better be obeyed, and *schnell*, too. Whatever it was that Sisera said to Jael that afternoon, it must have had something like the emotional effect of *"Juden heraus!"* shouted in the streets of a small village in eastern Poland.

History is rich in examples of Siseranism. The language of the Cro-Magnons must have had upon the Neanderthals the same effect as Norman French had upon the English after 1066. Furthermore, it isn't only the victors and the vanquished who dwell together speaking different tongues. The war doesn't really go on forever. When the fighting is over — for a while — the victors and the vanquished often settle down to become the rulers and the ruled. They continue to speak different languages. Their languages may in time merge and become one, but they will still find a way to speak different languages. That is the case with us.

The arrangement offers some advantages on both sides. The powerful can write the laws and the rules in their own language so that the weak come before the courts and the commissions at a double disadvantage. (You'll see what that means when they audit your tax return.) The ruling class also becomes the "better" class, and its language must be the language of literature and philosophy and science and all the gentle arts. The subjects, whose language is deemed insufficiently elegant or complex to express such matters, are thus excluded from the business of the intellect in all its forms and relegated to tradecraft and handiwork, for which their rudimentary babble is just about good enough. On the other hand, the rudimentary babble of the riffraff is, after all, a language that the rulers don't, and generally don't care to, understand. The language of the subjects serves them as a form of "secret" talking, so that servants can mutter, not quite inaudibly, appropriate comments on the lord and his lady. It's the same kind of revenge that schoolboys used to take by learning fluent, rapid pig latin to use in the presence of pompous and pedantic masters.

The linguistic distinction between the rulers and the ruled seems so right, especially to the rulers, that where it doesn't occur naturally it gets invented. Thus the upper classes in Russia in the times of the czars were put to the trouble of learning French, a more "civilized" tongue, and reserved their Russian for speaking to servants, very small children, and domestic animals. Thus the French upper classes from time to time have gone through paroxysms of tortured elegance in language in order to distinguish themselves yet further from their inferiors. It would have seemed reasonable, and handsomely symmetrical, too, for the French aristocrats to have learned Russian, saving their French for servants, very small children, and domestic animals, but your standard everyday French aristocrat would rather drink out of his fingerbowl than learn a barbarous babble like Russian. It's interesting to notice that in both those cultures certain linguistic distinctions were ultimately obliterated, at least for a while, by bloody revolutions. True, there may have been some other causes as well, but these little lessons of history should cause at least an occasional sleepless night for those of our rulers who like to speak in a language not understood by the people.

We don't have two languages, of course, so those who rule us have the same problem that once troubled the French aristocracy. They have to devise an elaborate language-within-a-language that we can understand only sometimes and even then uncertainly. It is a mistake to think that the language of the bureaucrats is merely an ignorant, garbled jargon. They may not always know what they are doing, but what they are doing is not haphazard. It works, too.

We like to make jokes, for instance, about the language of the tax forms. Heh heh, we chuckle, ain't them bureaucrats a caution? Just listen to this here, Madge. Them bureaucrats, however, don't chuckle at all, and if you'd like to see just what the term "stony silence" really means, try chuckling at their jargon when they haul you down to the tax office to ask how you managed to afford that cabin cruiser. Even your own lawyer will start looking around for some lint to pick off his trousers.

And as long as we have a lawyer in view, ain't they something? We read with pitying shakes of the head the disclaimers and demurrers at the bottom of the contract. We like to imagine that we, just plain folks, are somehow, deep down where it really counts, superior to those pointy-headed word-mongers with all their hereinafters. Nevertheless, we do what they tell us to do. We always remember that if we can't figure out from their language what we're required to do, and if we therefore fail to do it, it isn't the writers of the jargon who will be called to account. Our sense of superiority is an illusion, a convenient illusion from somebody's point of view; in fact,

172833

when we read the contract, we are afraid. It is the intent of that language to make us afraid. It works. Now *that* is effective writing.

Imagine that the postman brings you a letter from the Water and Sewer Department or the Bureau of Mines or some such place. Any right-thinking American will eye even the envelope in the same way he would eye some sticky substance dripping from the underparts of his automobile. Things get worse. You open the letter and see at once these words: "You are hereby notified . . ." How do you feel? Are you keen to read on? But you will, won't you? Oh, yes. You will.

Here comes another letter. This one doesn't even have a stamp. It carries instead the hint that something very bad will happen to any mere citizen caught using this envelope for his own subversive purposes. You open it and read: "It has been brought to the attention of this office . . ." Do you throw it out at that point because you find it too preposterous to think that an office can have an attention? Do you immediately write a reply: "Dear So-and-so, I am surprised and distressed by the rudeness of your first ten words, especially since they are addressed to one of those who pay your salary. Perhaps you're having a bad day. Why don't you write again and say something else?" You do not. In fact, you turn pale and wonder frantically which of your misdeeds has been revealed. Your anxiety is increased by that passive verb — that's what it's for — which suggests that this damaging exposure has been made not by an envious neighbor or a vengeful merchant or an ex-girlfriend or any other perfectly understandable, if detestable, human agent, but by the very nature of the universe. "It has been brought." This is serious.

Among the better class of Grammarians, that construction is known as the Divine Passive. It intends to suggest that neither the writer nor anyone else through whose head you might like to hammer a blunt wooden spike can be held accountable for anything in any way. Like an earthquake or a volcanic eruption, this latest calamity must be accepted as an act of God. God may well be keeping count of the appearances of the Divine Passive.

Another classic intimidation with which to begin a letter is: "According to our records . . ." It reminds you at once, with that plural pronoun, that the enemy outnumbers you, and the reference to "records" makes it clear that they've got the goods. There is even a lofty pretense to fairness, as though you were being invited to bring forth *your* records to clear up this misunderstanding. You know, however, that they don't suspect for an instant that there's anything wrong in their records. Besides, you don't *have* any records, as they damn well know.

Such frightening phrases share an important attribute. They are not things that ordinary people are likely to say, or even write, to one another except, of course, in certain unpleasant circumstances. We can see their intentions when we put them into more human contexts: "My dear Belinda, You are hereby notified . . ." conveys a message that ought to infuriate even the dullest of Belindas. Why is it then that we are not infuriated when we hear or read such words addressed to us by bureaucrats? We don't even stop to think that those words make up a silly verbal paradox; the only context in which they can possibly appear is the one in which they are not needed at all. No meaning is added to "Your rent is overdue" when the landlord writes, "You are hereby notified that your rent is overdue." What *is* added is the tone of official legality, and the presumption that one of the rulers is addressing one of the ruled. The voice of Sisera puts you in your place, and, strangely enough, you go there.

We Americans make much of our egalitarian society, and we like to think we are not intimidated by wealth and power. Still, we are. There are surely many reasons for that, and about most of them we can do nothing, it seems. But one of the reasons is the very language in which the wealthy and powerful speak to us. When we hear it, something ancient stirs in us, and we take off our caps and hold them to our chests as we listen. About *that* we *could* do something — all it takes is some education. That must have been in Jefferson's mind when he thought about the importance of universal education in a society of free people. People who are automatically and unconsciously intimidated by the sound of a language that they cannot themselves use easily will never be free. Jefferson must have imagined an America in which all citizens would be able, when they felt like it, to address one another as members of the same class. That we cannot do so is a sore impediment to equality, but, of course, a great advantage to those who *can* use the English of power and wealth.

It would be easier to see bureaucratic language for what it is if only the governors and bureaucrats did in fact speak a foreign tongue. When the Normans ruled England anyone could tell the French was French and English, English. It was the government that might, rarely, pardon you for your crimes, but it needed a friend to forgive you for your sins. Words like "pardon" and "forgive" were clearly in different languages, and, while either might have been translated by the other, they still meant subtly different acts. They still do, even though they are both thought of as English words now. Modern English has swallowed up many such distinctions, but not all. We still know that hearts are broken, not fractured. This is the kind of distinction Winston Churchill had in mind when he advised writers to choose the native English word whenever possible rather than a foreign import. This is good advice, but few can heed it in these days. The standard American education does not provide the knowledge out of which to make such choices.

# 5

## "let's face
## it Fellows"

The Jiukiukwe have, you will remember, many different verb conjugations so that they may speak appropriately to their relatives. They have, also, all those words to designate every imaginable degree of relationship so that they will be able to choose exactly the right verb form to match those relatives. This seems to us quaint and curious and probably typical of a bunch of shiftless savages who haven't enough to do. Some similar system, however, is not at all unusual in languages. We have such a system in English, although it isn't always a matter of grammatical form and is much less complicated than the Jiukiukwe verb system.

People who speak the same language are always announcing not only their own membership in a society but also their recognition of the membership of others. When you present a paper to the Philosophical Association, you choose your diction and devise your sentences in such a way as to suggest that they haven't made too big a mistake in inviting you. When you are out boozing with your motorcycle buddies, you do the same. The choices are available in the language, and, just as well as the Jiukiukwe, we can make our language match the social meaning of the occasion upon which we speak. For them, the language works well because it can make the distinctions important to them: familial distinctions. For us, the language works well because we can make the distinctions important to us: social, educational, and economic distinctions. Those distinctions simply do not exist for the Jiukiukwe, and, just as we are amused by their vast vocabulary of family relationships, they would laugh at our swarms of words to make subtle distinctions in social, educational, and economic status.

It would bewilder them, for instance, to discover that there are words like "sofa" and "couch" that mean the same thing but that we use the one or the other according to our social status. They would find it hard to understand why we claim to have "correct" forms like "It is I" but feel perfectly free to say "It's me" under certain circumstances. They would marvel at our seemingly capricious use of our few surviving subjunctives and shake their heads at our extensive arrays of near synonyms among which we have to choose with delicate precision. When is a co-worker a colleague? When is a colleague an associate? When is an associate an accomplice? When is an accomplice a partner? When is a partner a sidekick? We know which word to use because these arrays of words point at cultural values familiar to us. The poor Jiukiukwe tribesman trying to learn English would ultimately have to learn our culture and all its unspoken values and beliefs before he could make such choices. This is true of anyone who undertakes to learn any language. Among other things, a language is an elaborate and complete display of the ideas of the culture that speaks it.

If you could ask a Jiukiukwe why he takes such pains to address his mother's only brother's eldest daughter in just that way, he would probably have to say that he does it because it's "right." He's right. That's why we do things like that too. They're right. They are "right," however, entirely in a social sense. Language is arbitrary, but it's not anarchic. Although there's no reason why this or that in a language should be "right" and something else "wrong," it does not follow that you can do whatever you please in it. At some point, of course, when you wander too far from what is "right" you'll cease to be intelligible. But long before you reach that point you will send out the news that you are not a member in good standing around here.

Politeness is not a special social refinement *added on, if possible,* to the everyday life of members of the same culture. It has its origin in something far more important than social convention, and it is expressed primarily in language, which serves to display the values of the culture. The origin of politeness is probably a religious feeling. One of the other worlds into which language points is the world of the numinous. It is in myth and legend, therefore, that we can detect the origin of politeness in language.

Imagine that you are reading a fairy tale. Here's a cocky young prince on his way to kill some monster who guards the water of life. The prince stops to eat his lunch in cool shade by a brook. A loathsome frog asks for a bite of his sandwich, but the hero will not lower himself to sup with a slimy amphibian and says so in as many words. Well, there's no doubt. He's going to come to a bad end.

When his younger brother comes by next year, however, he'll be glad to give that frog bites of his peanut butter sandwich, a little Kool-Aid, and even some polite chit-chat. You can just bet that that boy will bring back not only the water of life but a comely princess as well.

Behind this common theme lies the suspicion that the palpable world we see before us conceals other worlds from our view. What inklings we have of those worlds we have in the suggestions of our language, and it is in our language that we have access to those worlds. Almost every culture has a taboo against being rude to strangers. Ours has it, and a good thing too, or you'd never be able to find a bathroom in a department store. The purpose of this taboo seems to be to prevent us from saying or doing anything that might have some bad consequences for us in another world. You never know who a stranger *really* is, and it never hurts to be polite. In some cultures, even more care is taken, and woodsmen apologize to trees before they chop them down, and fishermen ask forgiveness of the fish. After all, what can you lose?

Our culture is not much concerned with the numinous, but in language we preserve many of the marks of a culture that *is*. We talk to animals and machines. We talk to teddy bears and tools. We say, of course, that we don't really mean to communicate with these things, but an anthropologist from another planet might not see it quite that way. We talk in different words, too, depending on how we are related to the persons we address. In this we are not different from the Jiukiukwe. We are different, however, in that we need more finesse in our language to get those modes "right" consistently, since we haven't the clearly visible grammatical apparatus in which to express them. All the Jiukiukwe have to do to speak in the proper fashion is to get their verb forms right. We have to do much more, not only in speaking "correctly" but in discerning exactly that mode of speech which is suitable to the circumstances. In fact, the task is so difficult that we often say "the hell with it" and speak any old way we can. Could they know this, the Jiukiukwe, and the extraterrestrial anthropologist as well, might conclude that we are a culture presently in the process of disintegration, a culture that no longer cares to represent its values in its language.

The Jiukiukwe who speaks his language accurately speaks it politely, that is to say, in precisely that way which best suits the context in which he speaks. Speaking so, he pronounces his allegiance to the values that hold his culture together. We do even more than that when we speak to each other, and especially when we write to each other, in a mode suitable to the context. Ours is, unlike the Jiukiukwe's, a highly technological society. To get this society through the day, more or less successfully, we have to perform with precision thousands and thousands of tasks. For us to proceed in good order requires a vast company of citizens at all social levels who are dependably accurate and precise in whatever job they may hire themselves out to do.

Accordingly, we have traditionally taught the young of this tribe certain disciplines intended to inculcate the habits of accuracy and precision. One such discipline, for instance, is mathematics. All schoolchildren ask, when they finally think to ask it, why they have to study things like geometry and algebra when any reasonable view of adult life reveals that grown-ups are not called upon to do geometry and algebra. In fact, grown-ups have all forgotten those things, as any child will discover when he asks for help with his homework. We used to answer that we taught them those things not so that they might *do* them in later life, although some few must and will, of course, but because such studies cause certain habits to form in the mind. Nowadays, we simply agree with the children that geometry and algebra are useless, and instead of wasting all that time we let them rap about interpersonal adjustment instead. This does not, somehow, make them "well adjusted," but it does provide that the techniques and devices that they will someday be responsible for won't be very well adjusted either. Even Steven.

Many similar habit-forming studies are possible in language. Consider spelling. Strictly speaking, there is no spelling in language. Spelling is peculiar to writing; language is a set of sounds and gestures. The sounds either make intelligible speech or they don't. The Jiukiukwe children don't study spelling, and, as things stand between us now, we would not be able to explain such a strange business to the Jiukiukwe at all. In fact, you can understand the social and technological importance of the study of spelling just by imagining all the things a Jiukiukwe tribesman would have to understand first before you could tell him why we make our children study spelling. Once he knew all that stuff, though, he would also be able to see the sense of studying other absurd things like punctuation and capitalization.

Furthermore, once he knew all that stuff, as we, of course, do, he might be able to see the social and technological meaning of this sad story: There was a young lady in Pennsylvania who was incensed when she found two typographical errors and even an error in grammar in her local newspaper. Fortunately for the course of Western culture, she knew the right thing to do, and she did it. She fired off a stiff note of protest to the editor. And who better to do it? She was, after all, a schoolteacher, and rightly mindful of the baleful influence of the popular media on her impressionable charges.

Among other things, she wrote: "In writing I teach my third graders to proofread their work and I don't expect them to find all mistakes. But, let's face it Fellows you are not 8 and 9 year olds and this artical should have never gotten past you let alone printed in the form it was." That's what she wrote. Those are her words, her syntax, her punctuation, her capitalization, her spelling. Her spelling of "artical" appears in three more places, so it's no fluke, and in one place the word "allowed" comes out as "aloud."

Here's another sad story: Your car has broken down at night in a strange town in Alabama, perhaps. A man who claims to be a mechanic is trying to find the spark plugs. You point them out, but he is unable to remove them because he is turning the wrench the wrong way.

Here's an even sadder: Just as you are about to sink into unconsciousness in the operating room, you hear the surgeon asking the nurse which of those doohickeys are the clamps. Good luck to you. Good luck also to a batch of third graders out in Pennsylvania.

The schoolteacher's errors are what we call "small." An equivalent failure of technique in the man who has checked your airplane might be something like forgetting to tighten one lousy little bolt. There may well be a good chance that this trivial oversight will *not* kill everybody on board, depending on exactly which bolt it was. But who knows? Airplanes are very tricky devices, and there may well be some bolt or other that had damn well better be tightened if the contraption is to fly. However, when a schoolteacher writes "artical" for "article" and overlooks a few silly little commas, her students do not at once crash to earth in flames. Not at once.

There is a sense in which her children don't have to study English at all. Even third graders can say very complex things, quite understandably, without having, or needing, any notions at all about grammar and spelling. When we do set about to teach them a language in which they are already at home, perhaps even fluent, we have two things in mind. One of them is a social goal: a social goal not much different from what we have in mind when we teach them to use knives and forks at the table. Children who grow up without having learned to use knives and forks at the table may be charming and valuable human beings, but they will often be passed over for promotion. Furthermore, it seems unlikely that only *that* portion of their rearing could have been neglected. When you have lunch with a man who eats his lasagna with his fingers, you have reason to suspect that he may have one or two other social deficiencies.

Accordingly, we try to teach our children to spell correctly because, for one thing, they'll look bad if they spell incorrectly. It may, in the course of their lives, even cost them money if they can't spell. As things are with us, we would generally like our children to make more money rather than less, if only because so many of us are supported by the taxes other people pay. But it's more than that, of course; bad spelling just isn't respectable. You may, perhaps, want to lament this fact. You are free to do so. The fact remains.

Consider the social consequences that might be visited on that third-grade teacher. Suppose your child were in her class — the chances of this, by the way, are about even. There she is, that teacher who teaches her third graders to proofread their work, loftily not expecting them to find all their mistakes. Are you confident that she would be able to see whether or not they *had* found all their mistakes? We know one thing: She wouldn't be able to see that one of her students misspelled "article." She seems likely, also, to be unable to distinguish between "aloud" and "allowed." She will certainly be confused, and without knowing that she is confused, about some conventional punctuation and capitalization.

Does it seem possible that those two words — "article" and "allowed" — are the *only* words that she can't spell, and that it was only a calamitous coincidence that they happened to appear in her letter? It does not. A person who can misspell "article" and "allowed" can probably misspell something else. Would that something else be one other word? No, it would be more than one other word. Two? Ten? Seven hundred fifty-three? Does it matter? It does not.

What does matter is that you — remember, you're still supposing that your child is in her class — can now pick up the phone and call your neighbor down the street, the one you voted for last November when he was elected to the school board. You can don righteous indignation or mild bewilderment or anything in between, but, however you do it, you'll be able to speak as one having knowledge. *You* know how to spell those words, right? So what the hell is going on here? Who hires these people? Where do they come from? What could be more satisfying than a legitimate and documented complaint against those people in the schools who tell us so haughtily that they know what they're doing?

The questions are good ones. Who *does* hire teachers who can't spell? Where *do* they come from? The questions grow more ominous the more we think about them. Just as we suspect that this teacher's ineptitude in spelling is not limited to those two words, so we must suspect that she has other ineptitudes as well. We see already that her education has been less than perfect. Is her knowledge of arithmetic, for instance, also less than perfect? How well informed is she about history and science? Those very misspellings — don't they seem characteristic of a person who simply hasn't done much reading? That is, after all, the way most of us learn to spell correctly. When you've seen "allowed" and "aloud" thousands of times on the page, you just know which is which. And if this teacher hasn't done much reading, how likely is she to be well informed about history and science, or any of those things in which we expect her to instruct our children?

Well, who *did* hire her? Some principal, presumably, or some committee, or somebody. Let's imagine that it was a committee. What did they look for in her credentials? In her letter of application, were there errors? Would the members of the committee have been able to detect them? Would some of them say, even now, that a silly misspelled word here and there is too trivial to worry about?

And where *did* she come from? Some school graduated her, and some board granted her a certificate to teach. Did she just slip through the cracks in the system? Is she the only member of her class, the only graduate of her college, whose spelling is shaky? Of all of those teachers and incipient teachers, is she the only one who doesn't seem to have done much reading? The professors who wrote her references — did they mention that she had some problems with spelling? Did they *know* that she had some problems with spelling? Had they read any of her writing? Did she *do* any writing? As much writing as she did reading, perhaps? If your physician's elementary training in anatomy were as uncertain as this teacher's spelling, would you think it too trivial to worry about?

This is not a quiz; don't answer any of those questions.

For now, leave it at this: If social acceptability is one of the goals of the study of English, it will be but poorly served by this teacher and, it seems, just as poorly served by the system that made her a teacher. But there is another more important goal in mind when we subject children to the study of a language they already know. It is the habit of correctness and precision.

# 6

# Trifles

Those who have the habit of correctness and precision can do things by design; those who don't usually have to depend on luck. And when we fly in airplanes or undergo surgery or file our tax forms, we feel better if we can depend on something more than luck. It isn't luck that rings the right phone in Honolulu — it's simply correct dialing. (Getting a dial tone is luck.) We are a notably superstitious people, but we aren't superstitious enough to believe that our keys fit our locks by a marvelous stroke of good fortune. Our world is more and more crowded with things that will work only if lots of people have been correct and precise. That they seem to work less often and less well is a sad fact directly related to the third-grade teacher who can't spell. Here are some other people who can't do things:

In May of 1978 the executive secretary of the Michigan Board of Pharmacy wrote, in a letter to a Michigan physician: "Costs of administration of the act is considered and controlled substances fees merit an increase because of administration costs."

A Department of Transportation manual suggests that "If a guest becomes intoxicated," you might "take his or her car keys and send them home in a taxi."

George Washington University offers after-hours courses for the convenience of federal employees. Among its offerings you can find "Business and Proffessional Speaking," and "Effective Writting." The latter is a noncredit course, which is some consolation.

What do such small errors mean? What do we know when we see that a high-ranking government official cannot, invariably, make his verbs and subjects agree? Do you suppose that *he* is as tolerant of small errors in other matters as he would probably want us to be in this matter? Would he say of equivalent mistakes in his bank statement: "Well, a dollar here, a dollar there — it's just a little mistake"?

And the instructor who is going to teach that course in Effective Writting — will he ignore, should he ignore, silly mistakes in spelling in his students' papers? After all, English spelling is notoriously difficult. Should we recognize that "writting" is just a careless error, a slip of the finger, a minor and momentary lapse? Are mistakes of this order worthy of serious concern?

Yes.

It is true that English is a difficult and complicated language. It is also true that, like any language in regular use, it's always changing, perhaps very slowly, but changing. Nevertheless, in some way it is simple and permanent enough so that anyone who uses it can safely spend his whole life using singular verbs to go with singular subjects and plural verbs to go with plural subjects. That's what English does, and some call it correct. Sometimes we don't know whether a subject is singular or plural: Is the enemy retreating or are the enemy retreating? That's one of the things that make English entertaining, but it's not very important. There's no question, however, about "costs," and when the executive secretary of the Michigan Board of Pharmacy says that costs is considered, he is wrong. He has not been overcome by the awesome complexities of the English language, he has not failed to find the appropriate expression of a complicated idea, he has not violated the metaphoric consistency of his letter, he has simply made a mistake. It's not much of a mistake; it's something like the mistake a pharmacist might make when he gives you the wrong pills.

Of course, we take the pharmacist's mistake more seriously, since it might result in sudden death or at least convulsions. But the executive secretary's mistake is still an example of careless imprecision which, in this case, has simply not resulted in sudden death or convulsions. For the concerns of our society, though, the executive secretary's mistake is *more* significant than the pharmacist's. It suggests that a man in an important position, a functionary of government, is careless and thoughtless in doing his work and that he seems not to have learned the habit of precision and correctness.

Look again at what he has written: "Costs of administration of the act is considered and controlled substances fees merit an increase because of administration costs." Even our third-grade teacher could probably point out that the poor fellow was confused because the word that precedes the verb is "act." Nevertheless, it isn't the *act* that's being considered, it's the *costs,* so we say that they *are* being considered. There, that's not so hard, is it? So how could an executive secretary make a silly little mistake like that? He probably just wasn't paying attention, that's all, and his friends would surely say that just as though it were an excuse. But it isn't an excuse; it is simply an explanation. If he wasn't paying attention to what he had to say, to what *was* he paying attention? Isn't it his job to pay attention to his job? Isn't it part of his job to write letters to physicians who ask questions? Is this the only time he has failed to pay attention?

Difficult as English is in many ways, this is one way in which it is not difficult: It's not only possible, it's easy, to find the right verb to go with "costs." An executive secretary who fails in this ought to be as unthinkable as a statistician who subtracts 6 from 9 and gets 2. If a statistician or your computer at the bank subtracted 6 from 9 and got 2, you would not feel mildly irritated and amused. You'd ask what the hell is going on here, and you'd become deeply suspicious, wondering what the hell *else* is going on here. If this work is incorrect in such a small and easy matter, it seems likely that it will contain mistakes in large matters, large mistakes for which we would never have looked if we hadn't seen the small one.

When we look again at the executive secretary's sentence, we see that the silly little mistake, as bad as it is, is only a tiny indicator of a much larger failure of precision. Even provided the correct verb, his sentence says that costs of administration are considered and that these fees have to go up because of costs of administration. Why does he say the same thing twice? Is it because he doesn't have to pay for the paper or the typist's time? Is it because he is still thinking about something else and doesn't notice? Could it be because his case is weak and needs empty reiterations?

That unfortunate executive secretary has made a little mistake, a mistake much narrower than a church door, but 'tis enough, 'twill serve. Unfortunately, though, if you ask for him tomorrow, you won't find him a grave man. You'll just find him.

Not many years ago, it was a popular sport to collect and publish silly mistakes made by schoolchildren in their compositions. Many books of these so-called boners were printed for the delectation of grown-ups who laughed and chuckled. "Heh, heh, ain't they cute." Sometimes venturesome publishers went even further and printed collections of idiocies from the notes that schoolchildren brought from home. These were usually pathetic examples from barely literate people, but we chuckled and laughed some more. Now, like desperate drillers looking for new pockets of gas, we publish collections of the pomposities and malapropisms of politicians and bureaucrats. Again we chuckle and laugh. We don't find them quite as cute as those cunning kids, but still we laugh. It makes us feel superior. And because we feel superior we forgive; and we're willing to believe that a member of the city council, say, or a senator, shouldn't be judged too harshly merely by the inanity of his words. We'll still reelect him. After all, anybody can make a mistake. We make *this* mistake because it does not occur to us that there is no other way to judge the work of a mind except through its words, and we pay attention only long enough to be amused. In fact, however, those silly little mistakes always mean something important.

That line from the Department of Transportation means something. It's funny, right? "If a guest becomes intoxicated . . . take his or her car keys and send them home in a taxi." Heh, heh. We imagine the conversation: "Uh, listen, would you, uh, mind taking these keys to, uh, Four Seventy-one Laurel Street, driver?" "The keys? You want I should drive them keys to Laurel

Street?" "Yeah, you see, well it doesn't matter, I mean, just take these keys . . ." "Look, Mac, it's late. What is this? Some kinda gag or something?" Very funny.

It's so funny that we don't discern the failure of mind that has caused that silly mistake. It's a miniature example showing how ideology numbs the brain and forbids precision. While we're giggling at the car keys going home in the taxi, we forget all about that "his or her" business. The writer of this sentence was so worried about a possible charge of sexism that he lost the power of rational thought and speech. He had to say "his or her" because a simple "his" would have been one of those now unacceptable forms, and because we are now required to assert that women are also people and even that they are just as likely as men to get drunk. So there. Having implied all that, however, and most ungallantly, if you ask me, the writer had made himself a problem. Could he say "take his or her keys and send him or her home in a taxi"? He could not. First of all, it sounds lousy — let's give him credit for recognizing that. Second, and maybe he didn't recognize this, that would be a clever, satiric comment on the motive that inspired "his or her" in the first place. It would have made a silly form sound even sillier. So, what to do? Ah, of course. When in doubt about those personal adjectives and pronouns, pluralize! Plurals have no sex. It's every person for theirselves!

So we get "send them home in a taxi" and we think it's funny. It is, however, the sign of a failure to solve a problem. It's not a very big problem, and the solver, or the should-be solver, is someone who is hired and paid by the taxpayers to solve just such problems, even should they be hard. What could have been in his mind? Could he have been worried that his boss would get a stiff note from Gloria Steinem insisting that the Department of

Transportation take due note of the fact that women also get drunk? Could he or she have feared that his or her boss would call him or her on the carpet? Or could it have been simple ignorance?

This example is more portentous than the executive secretary's verb. Like the third-grade teacher's letter, this is an example of a corporate failure. Those car keys showed up in a published and widely circulated manual. You and I paid for it. We paid for the compiling, the writing, the rewriting, the editing, the proofreading, and everything else. How many people were involved in letting this silly mistake out into the world? Two things are possible. Not one of them noticed, or at least one of them noticed. If nobody noticed, we're being served by a pack of careless ignoramuses. If somebody noticed, then at least one of them is not a careless ignoramus but some kind of cynical elitist, I guess, who says, What the hell, your ordinary citizen in the street doesn't have enough brains to see the difference — let it stand. And, he, too, might also have been a little bit afraid of Gloria Steinem.

The third of these examples is surely the most trivial, but just as surely the most interesting. There they are, those thoughtful intellectuals, those bearers of the glowing lamp of learning down at George Washington University. Gladly they give their time and expertise to struggling federal file clerks hoping to rise in the world. It's a good way to pick up an extra buck, too. And just look — undone by a typist! "Business and Proffessional Speaking." "Effective Writting." Great. Can't you just see some silly twit, chewing gum, thinking about a new hairdo, casually typing some *f*'s and some *t*'s? Look behind her. See the silly twit who reads what she has typed and sends it out. And that poor sap who has to teach the course in "Effective Writting," what's he going to say at the first class meeting? You know what he's going to say, don't you, *if*, that is, he knows the difference and *if* any of his eager students know the difference. He's going to be funny. "Heh, heh, well, I guess we can all see why we need to have a course like this, eh?"

Everyone knows that English spelling is difficult. People who speak English are always looking up words in dictionaries, a practice uncommon among speakers of most other modern languages. We actually have annual nationwide contests in which scrubbed children perform like well-trained seals and outdo one another in spelling nifty and almost utterly useless words from "abiogenetic" to "zymurgy." We have devised elaborate rules in mnemonics, only to devise further mnemonics to deal with the exceptions and even the exceptions to the exceptions. Crackpots ranging from George Bernard Shaw to the man who opened the first All Nite Diner have undertaken to "fix" our broken spelling. So far, nothing has worked. The next logical step is simply to give up. Let her spell it "writting" even "ritting," who cares? We all know what she means, don't we?

But the question is not: Can we understand this typist? It is: How did this typist come to be, and what does this mean for us all? There are, it happens, some ways in which the spelling of English is perfectly regular and easy to learn. Any fool can see quickly enough that that double consonant in "knitting" is one of the few, grudging accommodations that written English makes to spoken English. One of the wonders of English is the way the written and the spoken (writen and spokken?) forms do disregard each other. Like distant cousins long alienated by a family feud, each goes its own way as though the other didn't exist. It's a rare treat to find them in agreement. But who *does* find them in agreement? People who speak English? No. Their agreement is not visible to people who speak English; it is visible, and often and regularly visible, only to people who *read* English. Making this distinction in written English is automatic to people who have done some reading. But to those for whom that double consonant business is nothing more than a statutory precept left over from the seventh grade, the distinction is not always available. For such, the distinction between "writing" and "writting" is a matter of luck. We may have to conclude that this unhappy typist is ill-educated and poorly read.

There is, however, another possibility. It may be that she is, in fact, an uncompromising ironist. Can it be that she was given a piece of paper from which to type this bit? Of course. And on that piece of paper, could someone *else*, the Dean of Extension Studies, say, have written "writting"? Perhaps she said to herself, between her teeth, "Aha. The stupid boob has done it again. Good. Let him eat it." An engaging fantasy, but deans, of course, don't make mistakes in spelling. The girl will have to take the rap. She'll have to take the rap for "proffessional" too. After all, deans *are* professional. If there's one word they know how to spell, that's probably it, even though "professional" isn't quite as easy to do as "writing."

Those of us who know how to spell "professional" — how did we learn? It wasn't hard. Most of us just had occasion to look at the word often enough as we read. But there's some logic in this spelling, too. Any thoughtful mind can figure out that profession, like confession, is some kind of fession, whatever *that* may be. And a thoughtful mind notices, too, that pro and con are familiar; we can even find them in company if we can think a minute and come up with "provoke" and "convoke." We don't even have to know how to voke to see

elements making structures in some logical fashion. So —
in "professional" pro is added to fessional. Easy. You
don't have to know any Latin, you don't even have to
know that there is such a thing as Latin, to figure out
how to spell "professional." All you need is a working
mind and the ability to see likenesses and a little store
of examples. Well, not quite. You also need to have
looked at the word enough times so that something will
seem wrong when you see "proffessional." That's the
hard part, because it needs the habit of reading.

So how much does it matter? These fry are all very
small. And if they can't read or write much, who cares?
So some people make mistakes. Well, try not to think
about them for a while. Think instead about the president of the University of Arizona, a big fry, who writes
as follows in the magazine sent out to alumni:

> As has been the case for the past several years, the
> most notable accomplishment of the University during
> 1976–77 was the strides took toward recruiting distin-
> guished faculty members. Never before have so many
> outstanding scholars, teachers, and researchers joined our
> institution. These men and women are the very lifeblood
> of the University. They will hasten the time the uni-
> versity reaches its goal of true excellence.

If some of those outstanding scholars read the alumni
magazine, they may want to hasten something else, but
their chagrin will be small compared with that of those
faculty members who've been around for more than a
year. They've just been excluded from the lifeblood, the
*very* lifeblood. Strangely enough, though, even the new
faculty, the very lifeblooders, are given only second place
because the "most notable accomplishment" is not, in

fact, their additions to the roles, but the "strides took toward recruiting" them.

What a pity. That little paragraph is full of padding and clichés, but that's what we expect from presidents of all kinds. Their appearances, after all, are mostly ceremonial, and they are expected to mouth empty and generally comforting formulae. The president's message is like the interminable benediction of the with-it young clergyman, emanating Brut, who has been invited for the first time to the monthly dinner meeting of the Kiwanis. Who listens? We expect clichés. We expect compounded clichés in which *mere* lifeblood is barely thicker than the punch; it has to be *very* lifeblood. Excellence? Just excellence? Certainly not. Down there in Arizona it's *true* excellence or nothing. Faculty are always distinguished, scholars are always outstanding, accomplishments always notable, time always hastened, and strides always took.

Would you like to be the president of a large university? It's fun. And, at least in some ways, it's obviously no more difficult than being a third-grade teacher or even a typist. Maybe a university president does have to cultivate the good will of wealthy benefactors so that his life probably isn't as interesting as a typist's life; nevertheless, the standards of precision and correctness are the same for both. In both the typist and the president we expect and find the same kind of workmanship — a little bit shoddy. The typist and the president, just like the teacher and the executive secretary, and the people at the Department of Transportation, are products of a pretentious but shoddy education. It's the pretensions that make it shoddy.

Our educators, panting after professionalism, are little interested in being known for a picayune concern with trifles like spelling and punctuation. They would much rather make the world into a better place. They have tried on the gowns of philosophers, psychologists, and priests. That's why, when they think of their "teaching goals," they say those things in the questionnaire. They see themselves as guides to emotional development, instigators of creative capacities, and molders of moral character. When they *must* attend to the factual content of some subject, they prefer to say that they impart that "general insight into the knowledge of a discipline." Niggling details, like spelling and punctuation, seem base by contrast with those noble goals. Our educators have established for us what may be a genuinely new kind of cultural institution — although it is something like the Austro-Hungarian Empire — that stubbornly avoids those undertakings in which it might succeed and passionately embraces those in which it must probably fail.

# 7

## The
## Columbus Gap

American public education is a remarkable enterprise; it succeeds best where it fails. Imagine an industry that consistently fails to do what it sets out to do, a factory where this year's product is invariably sleazier than last year's but, nevertheless, better than next year's. Imagine a corporation whose executives are always spending vast sums of money on studies designed to discover just what it is they are supposed to do and then vaster sums for further studies on just how to do it. Imagine a plant devoted to the manufacture of factory seconds to be sold at a loss. Imagine a producer of vacuum cleaners that rarely work hiring whole platoons of engineers who will, in time, report that it is, in fact, true that the vacuum cleaners rarely work, and who will, for a larger fee, be glad to find out why, if that's possible. If you discover some such outfit, don't invest in it. Unfortunately, we are all required to invest in public education.

Public education is also an enterprise that regularly blames its clients for its failures. Education cannot, after all, be expected to deal with barbarous and sometimes even homicidal students who hate schools and everything in them, except, perhaps, for smaller kids with loose lunch money. If the students are dull and hostile, we mustn't blame the schools. We must blame the parents for their neglect and their bad examples. If the parents are ignorant and depraved, then we must blame "society." And so forth — but not *too* far. Those who lament thus seem not inclined to ask how "society" got to be that way, if it *is* that way, and whether or not public education may have made it so.

The theme of the educators' exculpation, in its most common terms, goes something like this: We educators are being blamed for the corporate failures of a whole society. Our world is in disarray, convulsed by crime, poverty, ignorance, hatred, and institutionalized materialism and greed. The public expects us to cure all these ills, but that's just impossible. We are being given a bum rap. Besides, we're not getting enough money to do the job.

Well, it is a terrible thing to be held accountable for the sins of the world, and even worse that such a fate should be visited on such a noble and self-sacrificing bunch. We'd all feel much better, surely, if we could only pin all the pains and disorders of the human condition on some institution better suited to take the rap — General Motors, perhaps, or the Mafia. Come to think of it, however, General Motors never claimed that it could cure those pains and disorders; even the Mafia was not so bold. Public education *has* made such claims.

Our educators have said that they would teach love and the brotherhood of mankind as well as the importance of brushing after meals. They have promised to teach social consciousness and environmental awareness, creativity, ethnic pride, tolerance, sensitivity to interpersonal/ intercultural relationships, and the skills of self-expression, provided, of course, that such skills didn't involve irrelevant details like spelling and the agreement of subjects and verbs. They have said that they will straighten everybody out about sex and venereal disease and the related complications of family life, and about how to operate voting machines and balance checkbooks. They have invited Avon ladies to rap with third graders about their career objectives. They have undertaken to engender in naturally self-centered and anarchic children a profound respect for the folkways of migrant workers and the peculiarities of octogenarians. All of this, and much more, they promise us.

General Motors did not presume to promise us those things. Even the Mafia, perhaps the only enterprise in the country that could actually achieve such results in its own peculiar fashion, refrained from making such offers. Unlike public education, General Motors and the Mafia are modest, medium-sized enterprises fully aware of their limitations. Furthermore, each of them, in its own way, does have to do some palpable work for its money, but public education is guaranteed a handsome income whether it works or not. In fact, the less it works, the larger the income it can demand. What kind of nation would this be, after all, if we refused to invest more and more money in the pursuit of such noble and splendid goals?

Very few Americans will recall asking the educators to pursue such goals. It was the educators who decided not only that such an enterprise was mandated by the people but that it belonged properly in the public schools. They are experts, right? Who are we to say what they should or shouldn't — or could or couldn't — do? Who are we to go against the will of the people? Anyway, all of those things are just wonderful. It is possible, though, that we wouldn't now be blaming educators for not doing them if they hadn't assured us that they could and would do them. We hold no grudge against the crackpot next door who is working on a perpetual-motion machine unless he has told us that he could make one and separated us from lots of our money to buy custom-made magnets and extra-large rubber bands.

Most of us *will* recall that somewhere in our history, maybe it was back in Jefferson's time, we *did* ask the schools to teach everybody to read and write and cipher. Somehow, as hard as it may be to teach those things, it does seem a more modest undertaking than teaching love and tolerance and the brotherhood of all mankind. We may have expressed a few other desires — that the children should learn something of history, their own history especially, and of the literature and art that have not solved the ills of the human condition at all, but have made them clear and concrete and all too human. We did hope that the children would learn something of science and its methodology, by which we can understand and work at least some of the things in the world. We did ask a few other little things, most of them matters of fact and knowledge, silly things sometimes, like the names of the states and their capitals, and the length of the Nile and the Amazon, and the author of Gray's "Elegy."

Those few things that we do seem to have asked of public education are remarkably possible to teach. It is faddish nonsense to say that we don't know how, for instance, to teach reading and writing to the ignorant and must spend lots of money on studies and experiments before we can begin. All children are ignorant. All children who have ever learned to read and write have begun that task in ignorance. We know how to teach reading and writing — it's been done successfully millions and millions of times. It does require exactitude and discipline, and somewhat more of those things in the teacher than in the learners. It requires drill and recitation and memorization and practice, but these things can be made to happen. In one way, it is easy to teach reading and writing and arithmetic because it's possible to achieve concrete and measurable results through regular and practicable methods. In that respect, it is very difficult to teach the brotherhood of all mankind because we don't know exactly what that is or how we would measure it. In another way, however, it's much harder to teach reading and writing and arithmetic because we do have to know those things if we are to teach them, and we do have to be continuously rigorous and exact. To teach the brotherhood of mankind seems to be mostly the presentation of attractive but untestable assertions and the re-iteration of pious slogans and generalizations. If you'd like to be a teacher, but you don't want to work too hard, by all means set up as a teacher of the brotherhood of mankind rather than as a teacher of reading and writing and arithmetic. Such a career has the further advantage that no one knows how to decide whether you have actually taught anyone anything, whereas teachers of reading and writing and arithmetic are always being embarrassed when their students are shown not to have learned those things.

It takes a very simple fellow not to be a little suspicious when he notices that all this teaching of "values" and "attitudes" seems to be at once much easier and more profitable than teaching things like the chief exports of

New Zealand or the trade routes of the ancient Greeks, to say nothing of reading, writing, and arithmetic. Even an idiot will grow suspicious should he behold all of the implications of the values-teaching business. The profits are indeed enormous. You can't just go and teach values. You have to study *how* to teach values. You need money, and time, and questionnaires, and duplicating machines to duplicate the questionnaires, and keypunch operators to tabulate the replies to the questionnaires, and computer time to collate the data punched by the keypunch operators, and probably a new Mr. Coffee machine so that everybody can take a break once in a while. You need to figure out how to teach both the values themselves and the art of values-teaching to those who are eager to become values teachers. You need to devise the strategies by which values teachers can be sold to the schools in the disguises of social studies teachers and language arts teachers.

Here is how values-teaching works in the classroom. This is what they call a "values clarification strategy" — later on we'll have a sensitivity module. This values clarification strategy is suggested for use with students of all ages, and, as you'll see, it is equally relevant to the subject matter of any course taught in any school in America, which is to say, not at all.

The teacher writes two words — one at either end of the blackboard. "Cadillac" and "Volkswagen" are recommended; the first probably ought to go on the *right* end of the blackboard, thus suggesting, even in a home economics course, something useful about the eternal verities of politics and money. Having written "Cadillac" and "Volkswagen" in the neat block capitals that are actually *taught* in education courses, the teacher asks the student which of those brands they "identify with" and to get up and move to the corresponding side of the room. After some puzzled looks and shrugs, and one smart aleck in the back of the room drawing circles around his temple, and lots of milling and shuffling, the students end up standing in bunches on either side of the room, wondering what the hell can happen next. It's worse than they imagine, for the teacher now instructs them to choose partners of their own persuasion and to hold a serious discussion of the values that have sent them into the one camp or the other. The serious discussion is to last for two minutes. Then they all go back to their places and watch for the next pair of words.

Now you can imagine how they feel. It's like finding yourself at a party where a bubble-brained hostess wants everybody to play Truth or Consequences or else! Of course, even in the worst of our schools, there are no students as stupid as the teacher who would do such a thing, so they probably manage to find something less inane to talk about for those two minutes, giving thanks the while that at least it beats the Congress of Vienna or the square of the hypotenuse. Furthermore, if they shuffle back to their seats as slowly as possible, the bell might ring before they have to choose between a rose and a daisy or between an electric typewriter and a quill pen. Unlike the teacher, they know that anyone who "identifies" with an electric typewriter is crazy, just about as crazy as anyone who "identifies" with a quill pen.

Take a few moments wondering what it means "to identify" with a Cadillac. Only one thing is clear: the man who identifies with a Cadillac probably does not imagine that he *is* a Cadillac. Everything else is vague. It could be any or several of these: he wants a Cadillac; he admires a Cadillac; he deserves a Cadillac; he needs a Cadillac . . . add some more for yourself. The list will probably be very long and very boring. Without such a list of possibilities, however, the little game of values clarification would be impossible. The students and the teacher can play it only because they *don't* know what they mean by "identifying with" something. Nor is it the point of the game to *define* that term. The game is simply a self-indulgent wallowing in ignorance with only one clear result: It takes up some time that might have been spent in studying something concrete and useful but admittedly more difficult.

Grammar, for instance. Notice that such a futile exercise is made possible, and even made futile, because a transitive verb, "identify," has been twisted into an intransitive form. It is *not* a "rule" of English grammar that some verbs must have objects. It is simply the *fact* that some verbs evoke relationships that don't make any sense without an object. When someone asks you "How do we see?" you understand him well enough to answer, although the answer may be either a neurological disquisition or "through a glass, darkly." When he asks you "How do we view?" you need more information if you are to answer him, because the idea evoked by the word "view" is not complete in itself. This, like so many things that we think of as arbitrary rules, is actually a clue to how the mind works in English. The "identify with" values clarification game assures that, for a while at least, no mind will work.

Things like that really do happen in our schools. Although it may not seem so at first, it is just that sort of thing that causes the corruption of language that, in its turn, causes just that sort of thing. In fact, it is only the preachers and practitioners of such nonsense who take it seriously. Imagine for the moment that the students could be persuaded to take it seriously. There you are

— remember, this is suitable for all ages — standing on your side of the room. You *do* choose a partner, let's say, and you settle down to the serious business of discussing, for two minutes, the tremendous values and heartfelt convictions that have led you to identify with "Cadillac." What do you say? What *can* you say? No matter how seriously you take it, can you do much more than recite a slogan or two, put forth some well-known generalization, enunciate some vague impression or casual opinion? And your partner, obviously not in need of conviction, can do only the same. So there you stand, muttering desultorily about resale value and roominess and pointing out that a careful driver can save gasoline by not accelerating too fast. Great. Should you find yourself in such a predicament, of course, you *won't* take it seriously. Like any right-thinking human being, you will pick the best-looking partner you can reach and spend those two minutes arranging something for later. Now *that* might clarify some values. Vaporizing about Cadillacs can only air some prejudices, and not even strong ones at that.

Consider now what happens to language in an exercise like that. Are quill pens and electric typewriters values? To prize one, must we despise the other? Should we be doing any of this stuff at all in a school, where we are supposed to learn some arithmetic and the intelligent use of language? If a student is to take any learning at all from such an exercise, leaving aside the revelation that his teacher is a nitwit, it is that what we say doesn't much matter. Idle rapping is called the clarification of values. Any old thing at all, anything a teacher can *name*, becomes a value. Unreal polarities are suggested by the pairings of such "values," and students are given to understand that through discourse they have discovered that "value" in them that has led them to one pole or the other. This little game will hardly suggest to any student that a "clarification of values" must, if it is to take place at all, proceed through discursive statements and logical analysis. It leaves the impression that vague opinions and the suggestions of environment are "clarifications." Students usually *do* learn something in class, but it's seldom what the teacher had in mind. In this class, the students will learn to be content with empty talk and to accept random reflection as though it were knowledge.

This "values clarification" business is very popular in the schools, and an educationist named Simon has written, with a couple of pals, a nifty handbook chock-full of "values clarification strategies." The examples mentioned are not, as you probably thought, silly exaggerations — they're from the book. A wily teacher could spend a whole year playing those fun games in class and still have enough examples left over for summer session. They are all designed not only to stay as far as possible from hypotenuses but to reduce the power of language in the players. They achieve that result by offering the students experiences rather than study and feelings rather than knowledge. The experiences and feelings, however, exist as words only. It is hard to imagine the student suggestible and feebleminded enough to think that he does, in fact, feel more empathy for Arabs after eating a sheep's eye.

Eating a sheep's eye, of course, is not a values clarification strategy. It is what Simon would call a "sensitivity module," and here is a more likely example:

In teaching elementary children about the early world explorers, one teacher had her children go out and actually "discover" new parts of the city. One instruction was to "find a new and faster route to the ball field." The gap between the world of Columbus and their own world in the city was narrowed.

By "elementary children" he means, probably, children in elementary school, unless, perhaps, he thinks that "elementary" means something like "simple-minded." It would take a simple-minded child, indeed, to get sucked in to a silly project like this. And what makes the project silly is also what brought it to pass in the first place — bad language.

People who can use language accurately can make useful analogies and learn to understand things. They can also tell — through language, for there is no other way — just how far an analogy can be pushed before it becomes useless. That "sensitivity module" is drawn from a silly analogy, which suggests that what Columbus did is comparable to finding a better way to get to the ball field. To make such an analogy requires both ignorance and misunderstanding of history. That's not "discovery," and even Simon feels uncertain enough about it to put those quotation marks around the word. In fact, the search for some hitherto unimagined route to the ball field is so absurd on the face of it that the students who undertook it must surely have spent their time in the nearest snack bar. A teacher silly enough to give such an assignment has to be humored, of course, so the students must have spent a few minutes concocting a good story, maybe something about monsters and the edge of the known world.

Notice that this exercise is called a "sensitivity module." Such is the power of language that nonsensical time wasters like this become significant educational processes when given the right name, and money is spent to design them. In what sense this can be called a "module," there is no understanding. If this is a "module," then lunch might just as well be called a "module." In fact, lunch *is* a "module" in many schools. Just as in Dallas, buses are "motorized attendance modules." A module, therefore, is anything you please. There's no profit in worrying about the module, however; it's the "sensitivity" part that's important.

Schools are in favor of sensitivity and opposed, naturally, to insensitivity. In the traditional curriculum there are still some outdated things that cause insensitivity. Historical dates cause insensitivity. The square of the hypotenuse instills callousness. Untempered grammar and spelling produce ruthless elitism. The multiplication table can engender inhumanity, and precise diction has been known to result in fascism. Since we have not yet managed to persuade the public that such studies should be discontinued utterly, the best we can do is mitigate them, wherever possible, with expeditions into the mists of what is called noncognitive learning. If we make children learn mere facts about the difficulties of navigation in the fifteenth century, they may well grow up to be cutthroats and boors, totally lacking in sensitivity. Far better it is to send them wandering the streets of the city and pretending to search for *terra incognita.* That way, you see, they'll get the "feel" of exploration. Well, let's say that they can at least pretend to get the feel. When they get back, they won't know any dehumanizing things about the nasty economic implications of exploration in the Renaissance or those silly and irrelevant political struggles of fifteenth-century Europe, but they will have "narrowed the gap" between themselves and Columbus.

And what can that mean — to narrow the gap between us and Columbus? Those things that separate us from

Columbus — can they be taken all together and understood as a "gap"? If so, in what way, *exactly*, is the gap "narrowed" when we find a quicker way to get to the ball field? When we eat blubber, do we narrow the gap between us and the Eskimos? When we walk around blindfolded for an hour, do we narrow the gap between us and the blind? They do things like this in school — not just in the public schools but even and especially in the schools that produce the teachers for the public schools. All such "gaps" are very large and complex, and to understand them and to have knowledge about them will require that we first make many statements of fact. To "feel" like an Eskimo and to know what being an Eskimo involves are utterly different things. The former is probably impossible for non-Eskimos. The latter can be achieved by anyone who will attend to statements of fact. Ten thousand sensitivity modules will not teach us how it is with men who sail into the utterly unknown; to read their words just may give us an inkling.

People who worry about teaching sensitivity have little use for exactitude in statements of fact. The vagueness of narrowing gaps and identifying with Volkswagens seems to them somehow "humanistic," and precise statements of fact and matters of knowledge seem the opposite of "humanistic," whatever that might be. This attitude can survive and flourish only where language is diffuse and imprecise. The accurate statement of empirical propositions would destroy it.

It is possible, of course, to clarify values. Whether that is the proper business of the schools is another matter, but it surely can be done. It can be done, however, only through language, only through a chain of logical discourse. Logical discourse requires exactitude. If we *do* want to teach morality or at least the thoughtful examination of our deeds and their apparent meanings, we can do this only through teaching exactitude. It is no accident that thought, word, and deed keep company together in prayer books. To clarify our values must mean to make fine distinctions. To make fine distinctions means to see how different things are similar and how similar things are different. This calls for many finely tuned words and subtle grammatical devices and the ability to put them all together with precision. The finer the distinctions we can make in words and, therefore, in our thoughts, the finer the judgments we can make about the nature of our deeds. Contrariwise, careless and blunted words conceal the nature of our deeds.

I had read — and I believe it — that the Nazi bureaucracy generated thousands and thousands of pages of routine paperwork related to the business of killing Jews, but in all that paperwork the word "killing" appears nowhere. Those who think that a concern for precision in language is finicky and pedantic should ponder that for a while. The people who say to each other "Let's kill the Jews" have indubitably clarified their values. Having done so, they may find them repellent and decide to seek others, but I wouldn't count on it. The people who say that a sensitivity module will narrow the gap between us and Columbus have *not* clarified their values or anything else. If our values happen to be abhorrent, as they often are, we can know that only through stating them plainly. It's not impossible that thousands of Germans could have done what they did only because they spoke carefully of "transportation" and "resettlement" and "solution" rather than of "killing."

It is not only possible to clarify values but obviously desirable. It is also possible, and desirable, to balance budgets. To teach people how to balance budgets, it just isn't enough to let them play with fat wads of Monopoly money. We have to teach them arithmetic. To teach them how to clarify values, we must teach them mastery of the system with which we express values and the only device we have for "knowing" them. That's language.

The values of "values clarification" stand in need of some clarification. To *see* that requires enough skill in language to recognize the abuse of language. To *do* it requires even more. It would help, too, to remember the words of Hobbes: "For words are wise men's counters, they do but reckon with them; but they are the money of fools that value them . . . by authority." "Clarification" is a word. When a teacher in his authority tells his students that they will now clarify their values by rapping about Cadillacs and Volkswagens, what are the poor kids to do? They have not been taught the skills of language, and they have no choice but to believe or to pretend that they believe. In either case, they must grow up believing that the clarification of values is a silly game played in dreary places by preposterous people to no useful end. They become a herd and live, perforce, the unexamined life.

There is more clarification of values in a single sentence of Bacon than in all the strategies of Simon. Consider the rest of that line: "Reading maketh a full man; conference a ready man; and writing an exact man." We have read that line so often, of course, that we seldom do more than nod at it. When we give it some thought, we can discover (and this time the "discovery" is real) the power of that mind and the power of language in the meticulous choice of the words "full," "ready," and "exact." That's exact language and the expression of an exact thought. The words tell us not only that a well-read man is "full" but that an ill-read man is "empty," as empty as the student whose study of Columbus took him to the ball field. They tell us that the man who cannot "confer," who is not fluent and practiced in his speech, is uncertain and inept, like the student just returned from the ball field and needing desperately to convince his teacher that his sensitivity has been heightened — really! They tell us that the man who cannot "write" is imprecise and unclear in his mind, like Simon, who tells us that the Columbus gap has been narrowed through a sensitivity module.

There is no need, of course, to ferret out the fact that the schools are in the business of teaching "values" at the expense of reading, writing, and ciphering. They boast of it publicly. Here are the words of a professor of educational psychology explaining to the public why they ought to accept with equanimity the fact that students do so poorly on tests of reading, writing, and ciphering. Those tests, you must understand,

> do not attempt to quantify such crucial concerns as students' self-perception; their attitude toward, and relationship with, people whose culture and social class differ from their own; their ethical behavior, values, personal philosophy and moral commitments; their creativity, emotional health and sense of ethnic identity — precisely the areas that schools have been emphasizing.

So. We have traded skill in language and number for ethical behavior, personal philosophy, moral commitment, creativity, and emotional health. Not at all a bad deal. But wait. What has become of those millions of young people deeply schooled in morality? These are the "areas" the schools have been "emphasizing" for decades now. How is it that Earth is not yet fair and all men glad and wise? How is it that creativity and emotional health lead to the beating of teachers and the destruction of file cabinets? What personal philosophy calls forth the smashing of toilet bowls with sledgehammers?

Children are much smarter than we think. They know when they are being deceived and defrauded. Unless they can utter what they know, however, they know it only in part and imperfectly. If we do not give them the language and thought in which they might genuinely clarify some values, they will do their clarifying with sledgehammers. None of the lofty goals named above can be approached without the skillful practice of language and thought, and to "emphasize" those "areas" in the absence of that practice is to promulgate thought control rather than the control of thought.

# 8

## The Pill

Thought control, like birth control, is best undertaken as long as possible before the fact. Many grown-ups will obstinately persist, if only now and then, in composing small strings of sentences in their heads and achieving at least a momentary logic. This probably cannot be prevented, but we have learned how to minimize its consequences by arranging that such grown-ups will be unable to pursue that logic very far. If they were at home in the technology of writing, there's no telling how much social disorder they would cause by thinking things out at length.

Our schools have chosen to cut this danger off as close to the root as possible, thus taking measures to preclude not only the birth of thought but its conception. They give the pill to even the youngest children, but, just to be on the safe side, they give it to everybody else, too, especially all would-be schoolteachers.

Now find a comfortable position and read this miniature museum of contemporary American writing. These little essays were produced by college graduates applying for jobs as schoolteachers. The applicants may not have those jobs yet, but they do have certificates that attest to their competence and assure us that they have satisfied stringent requirements.

A. The use of behavioral objectives in a classroom are good because they help the teacher to see a more clear path for her/his teaching. He/she is able to predetermine what he/she will teach and hopefully at the end of that session the students will have learned what was outlined for them. Behavioral objectives can help the teacher evaluate her/his teaching by looking at them to see what has been accomplished in class. So many times, a teacher can get off of a subject and not realize the students are not learning the material they were designated to learn. If the students are aware of what they are to learn then they can make a greater effort to learn the information. The teacher may use the objectives as a form of evaluation for the students so that she/he may see how far they have progressed and whether or not the topic should be reviewed or more information can be added. Behavioral objectives are an overall good idea to help students and teachers see what direction the learning should be going in and how progress is being made.

B. In the process of teaching science to students there will be preassessment test to determine what the student already knows. From the finding of the preassessment test objectives, teacher and students will be designed. Concepts to be taught will be listed. If the subject area being covered is weather, than the different aspects of weather will be introduced. There will be worksheets and experiment to prove and evaluate the objectives for the activity. The activity children will be given activities that they will have to do on their own example collecting date of the formation of clouds and what weather usually follow certain cloud formation. The project must be flexable so that it meets the need of each child and is meaningful for them.

C. If I had a self-contained classroom with various children on different level, I would try to group them according to their abilities when working on certain subject matters. I would use behavior modification in my classroom in order to motivate the children. If we were working on math for example — If we were playing the bingo game (a game to help them recognize numbers) I would reward one person with a reward for bingoing if they could call out their numbers to me or if they couldn't remember a number I could help them and still they would bingo. I worked with some children in this and it really motivated them to learn because of the reward.

D. start with basic ways of setting & bumping the ball & controlling it — use drills of how many times before missing & others. set & bump ball against the wall — how to bump & set ball properly. demonstrate
start with different types of serves, find the one that suits them best & stick with it. keep eye on ball — Then start serving over the net. After that start placing the ball (determining where it's going to go. demonstrate so they'll know what I mean
start the spikers for taller individuals to spiking & setters in to setting ball close to net. Use fun games through out to keep them interested. demonstrate spiking
Cover the rules and go into game situation. Teach them how to dig for the ball & how to fall & avoid being injured.
Devide into equal teams & play games of volleyball best 2 out of 3. Use a tournament type play so that all teams will get a chance to play each other & if they're

pretty equally matched it will result in some very close & exciting games

Cover any questions the students might have & give them a handout of material that would be covered on a test. handout will include the things not to do & how to do them right.

That's what happens when you've spent four years popping little pills of jargon. Try to put down that nasty suspicion. It's just too much of a coincidence that all four of these teachers could have taken jobs in your local school system. One, maybe. Perhaps, just perhaps, even two. But all four? Impossible! Rest easy.

All of these passages are curious but instructive mixtures of ineptitude and technicality. Writer A, for instance, tells us that the use of behavioral objectives are good, revealing at one stroke a subtle knowledge of pedagogical theory and an inability to match subjects and verbs. The same writer shows an admirable abhorrence of sexism in all those slashed forms, even going so far as to give precedence now to one gender and now the other, but she/he seems confused about prepositions. The importance of this passage, however, is not to be found in such trivia.

Writer A may be confused about the rudiments of English, but he/she–she/he has clearly heard and practiced some jargon. This little essay is built on the assertion that there are such things as behavioral objectives and that they are "an overall good idea." If you've never before heard the term "behavioral objectives," count yourself lucky, but you certainly won't be mystified. Obviously, if we want someone to do something, that must be a "behavioral objective." In schools, adding up a column of figures is thought of as "a behavior," and getting students to do that is a behavioral objective. It's important to notice that adding them up wrong is, of course, also "a behavior," so that to teach children to add correctly becomes a matter of "behavior modification," but more of that later. There are lots of things that A didn't learn in college; some of them we can see, and from them we can infer many others. She/he–he/she *did*, however, learn a kind of vocabulary of special terms, each of which is used to conceal an emptiness of meaning and to make the obvious sound important. To what things or events in the world of experience does the term "behavioral objective" point? They are countless. If we persuade five-year-olds to latch their galoshes or convince a whole nation to convert its schools into gambling casinos, we have accomplished a behavioral objective. Should we fail, we have nevertheless promulgated behavioral objectives. In the language of the school people, an alarm clock would be called a mode of behavioral objective implementation, but so would a Christmas bonus or a thumbscrew. A term that means almost anything means almost nothing. Such a term is a convenient device for those who have almost nothing to say. We have to conclude that A heard about "behavioral objectives" very often in the teacher school — and somewhat less often about clear, precise writing and thinking.

Writer B cannot spell "flexible" or even "then" but has no trouble with "preassessment," a tricky word with lots of *s*'s. He cannot, however, make any sense of the word. Who could? "Preassessment" is something that can only happen before we have done any assessment, and we can preassess something just about as easily as we can pre-eat our breakfasts. The test referred to in B's first sentence might imaginably be called, if you must call it something fancier than just a test, a "pre-teaching" test. In contempt of sense, the "pre-ness" has been transferred to the assessing because it creates such a handsome word. The same principle, by the way, was at work in A, who promised to "predetermine what he/she will teach." You either determine something or you don't. Our language permits us to *say* things like "predetermine," or even "undetermine," and "subdetermine," but it doesn't let us mean anything by them.

Words like "preassessment" are paradoxical. They evoke an imagined world in which there is no sense or logic. To tolerate such words requires dullness of mind; to embrace them, lunacy. Most jargon, however, is something less extreme. We can see its normal attributes in B's use of the word "aspects"; "the different aspects of weather will be introduced."

Can't you just hear teacher B in class? "Dear children, I will now introduce an aspect of weather." What does he *do* then? What *is* an aspect of weather? What idea of the meaning of "weather" must we have if we are to separate it into its "aspects"? Is an aspect of weather a kind of weather — rainy, sunny? Is it a particular event like a hurricane? Is it an attribute of weather? Nice weather for ducks, for instance? Leaving weather aside entirely, what *exactly* is an aspect? Is "aspect," as so many seem to think, just another way of saying "phase" and "factor"? Is phase, perhaps, just one of the factors of an aspect? Can we divide just *anything* up into aspects or only certain kinds of things?

And, by the way, presuming against all odds that B does know what he means by "aspect," just what is involved in "introducing" it? To introduce an aspect, do you name it, or describe it? Do you, perhaps, as the word in fact suggests, stick it in? If "rain" is an aspect of weather, and that's probably what the poor fellow means, how do you go about "introducing" rain? And, for heaven's sake, why?

Writer C introduces — sticks in, that is — something called "behavior modification," an ominous aspect, no doubt, of the consequences of the preassessment of behavioral objectives. Teachers still put up with being called teachers, but they seem reluctant to admit that humble teaching is what they do. They prefer to modify behavior. Take a moment to go back and read again what C has written. Could you rest quietly, in the still watches of the night, knowing that C has been unleashed to modify the behavior of your children?

Aside from the obvious, which is far too comprehensive to have much meaning at all, what could "behavior modification" possibly mean? C says that he/she would "use" it to "motivate" the students. Is there some difference between behavior modification and the *use* of behavior modification, as there is a difference between a hammer and hammering? If so, how is the *use* of behavior modification to be distinguished from the act of modifying behavior any more than the use of a hammer is to be distinguished from a hammering? Isn't "motivating" itself a kind of behavior modification; and doesn't that sentence say that C will use behavior modification in order to modify behavior?

What it means is that C had come out of teacher school with his/her–her/his head full of empty terms. There is no doubt that C would also spell "preassessment" correctly, although she/he–he/she has a little problem with sentence structure.

There's no point in commenting in any detail on the words of D. It is worth remembering, however, that D is also a college graduate and a certified teacher. What's interesting is his touching faith in the "handout of material," a handout that will include, you will recall, "the things not to do & how to do them right."

Handouts of material are big business in Education. A typical class in Education starts with a handout of material, which handout provides nifty terms like "pre-assessment test" and "behavior modification." Then the class breaks up into small groups so that the students can rap and reach for themselves the conclusion that behavioral objectives are "an overall good idea." After four years of this, every graduating student walks into the world clutching thick sheaves of handouts of materials made up almost entirely of words and phrases that have little or nothing to do with real things or people or events in the world of experience.

# 9

# A Handout
# of Material

Jargon is a handout of material designed to prevent the need for thought. Consider the infamous "input." For certain technicians, this word has a concrete meaning and points to something that can be pointed to with no other word. For sales managers, deans, politicians, and most of the rest of us, "input" provides an ornamental cover for a hole in the brain. When a vice president for administration asks for your input, what *exactly* does he want? Does he want your opinion? Your advice? Your hypothesis? Your knowledge? Your hunch? Your money? What? Does he know? If he wants to know how many long distance calls you've made this month, why does that get called "input," the same term he would use in asking for your height, weight, and blood type? Does "input" describe adequately *anything* you might send someone?

Again, a word that means almost anything means almost nothing. The man who asks for your "input" is not put to the trouble of understanding what he wants. Furthermore, sometimes even bureaucrats and adminis- trators seem to be able to tell you what it is they actually do want. You get a letter from the district manager ask- ing for your hat size. He is making a study that will dis- cover whether skull capacity is related to monthly sales figures. Simple enough. But suddenly your hat size be- comes input. This isn't so bad; that number may in fact become part of what might technically be called "input." In his next letter, however, the same district manager asks if you think it's worth the trouble to keep the com- pany bowling league going for another year. And that becomes input. The word no longer makes any useful distinction.

Every craft has its technical lexicon, and the terms often make useful and necessary distinctions between one thing and all other things, sometimes exceedingly fine distinctions. The more technically demanding the craft, the more it needs an extensive and precise, technical lexicon. Contrariwise, crafts that make only small de- mands on the technical skills of their practitioners require only a small list of technical words and might even get by with none at all. The practice of some crafts, and schoolteaching seems to be one such, requires very little that could be called an organized technology. Such crafts ought not, therefore, to require much of a technical lexicon at all, but, strangely enough, it is often in just such crafts that we find the most elaborate jargon.

In our culture, technology commands admiration and respect. We love the nuclear physicists and the brain surgeons. We want to be like them when we grow up. Failing that, we'd like to be at least as technological as possible. One might imaginably draw a chart to rank our various callings in terms of their technological demands so that we could know whether to grant more respect to the systems analyst than to the forensic pathologist, but it isn't really necessary. We can always tell which of two crafts outranks the other by looking at its lexicon. Jargon runs only downhill. You will notice that although the educators have borrowed "input" from the computer people, the computer people have felt no need to borrow "behavioral objectives," or "preassessment" from the educators. It is a general principle that when A apes B it is because A thinks that B is better than A, although in the case of teenagers the opposite is true. Accordingly, we can conclude that educators and businessmen look up to military strategists, from whom they have borrowed "thrust," and to physicists and mathematicians, from whom they have borrowed "interface."

We like to think, or at least we like others to think, that what we do is important and difficult and that we achieve it only out of skill and intelligence. Since very few of our callings actually require much more skill and intelligence than the banging of trees with stones, we seize gratefully any opportunity to *sound* as though we were skillful and intelligent. Fortunately, such opportunities are frequent. All we have to do is listen to the people who really are, we think, skillful and intelligent. Consider the following remarks taken from an address to a faculty senate. The remarker is, or was, a provost, whatever that is. The title itself, of course, is another admission that academic administrators wish they had the skill and intelligence, to say nothing of the power, of high-ranking military officers.

This provost says: ". . . we are currently in a holding pattern as far as long-range planning is concerned." Now this shows us that provosts know in their hearts that air traffic controllers are more valuable and effective than provosts. It's true, of course, but the provost probably wouldn't want to assert it publicly. He speaks also of "a number of unanswered, unresolved issues which . . . provide a prelude to the onset of the process itself." This is more subtle. A prelude to the onset. Neither of these words is specifically the jargon of a craft, although "prelude" is vaguely musical and "onset" vaguely medical. Both sound quite concrete and specific, the words, as it were, of a man who knows what he's talking about. But the two of them together add up to an absurdity similar to "preassessment." The flavor is good, though; there's the whiff of aesthetic sensitivity in "prelude" and the hint of keen diagnostic power in "onset." Musicians and physicians clearly outrank provosts.

So do mathematicians. The provost gives them their homage in terms like "planning matrices" and "planning parameters." Hardly anyone who uses these words has any idea what they mean. It doesn't matter. "Parameters," except when used by those who do know what they are, is a useful omnibus word like "aspect," except that it's usually intended to point vaguely in the direction of some of the more remote aspects of something or other. "Matrix" is very popular these days. Polysyllables that end in $x$ have hypnotic power over the English-speaking mind. Strangely, that power is actually increased when the exotic $x$ disappears into an unlikely plural. People who can utter tricky plurals like "matrices" and "indices" (even trickier because of the disappearing $e$) must be very learned indeed.

So far, we can see from the provost's jargon that he feels inferior to air traffic controllers, musicians, physicians, mathematicians, and, perhaps, type founders and other craftsmen for whom a matrix is in simple fact a matrix. It is hardly surprising, since all those crafts are indeed more demanding than the craft of the provost. What is surprising, though, is that the provost also speaks of "variables which must be cranked into the decision model" and recognizes the need "to crank this kind of adjustment factor into the decision model" and even "to crank in some quality measures which speak to the level of teaching excellence." Whether out of inordinate modesty or ardent republicanism, the provost makes it clear that he stands in awe even of the technology of sausage manufacture. A handsome admission.

When there is no idea in the mind, a word rushes into the vacuum. This provost, for instance, speaks of the "need to recognize that there are a number of components in the process." "Components" is good, because it raises the provost, momentarily, to the rank of highly skilled professionals like the people who assemble Bearcat scanners, but the utterance is nevertheless disappointing. For one thing, almost anyone could have said it of almost anything. It's not likely to show up in future editions of *Bartlett's Quotations*. It reveals neither thought nor knowledge.

Imagine that you are chatting with Marco Polo, just back from Cathay, and you're burning to hear all about those strange people in a distant land. You ask what wonderful things he saw there; he tells you "marvels." You ask what the people wear; he tells you "attire." What do they grow; "crops." And their processes; what are they made of? "Components." Now you know all about Cathay.

When you divide a "process" into its parts, do you get "components"? Those who speak of components in a technical sense would probably say no. Components are generally discrete parts related to one another by the way they work in a system. The "parts" of a *process* might well have less distinct boundaries, and they are related to one another in a temporal or sequential fashion. A process takes place (sometimes) in a transmission, but the machinery is not the process. Well, couldn't we understand the "components of a process" as a metaphor? After all, we know what he means. We probably could, except that just a few sentences later he speaks of the same things as the "elements" of a process. While we're still trying to figure that out, he goes on to tell us about the "factors" of the same process.

Little wonder we're in a holding pattern circling above the prelude to the onset of this process. This is one hell of a process! Some of its constituents are components, some elements, and some factors. However, we know that that is not the case. Those are not designations of the different *kinds* of constituents; they are simply jargon terms that point to nothing in particular, and, therefore, to just about anything you please to imagine. So, come to think of it, *do* we know what he means? If he calls the constituents of this process, apparently at whim, components, elements, and factors, mightn't he just as well call them aspects, facets, and phases? Are all those words interchangeable for him? Probably. That means that he doesn't know what he means. If the process in question is at all complicated, this is probably not the man we want to set it going. He doesn't understand it, and he doesn't know how to go about understanding it. His jargon conceals, from him, but not from us, the deep, empty hole in his mind. He uses technological language as a substitute for technique.

The propensity for borrowed jargon is always a mark of limited ability in the technique of discursive thought. It comes from a poor education. A poor education is not simply a matter of thinking that components and elements might just as well be called factors; it is the inability to manipulate that elaborate symbol system that permits us to make fine distinctions among such things. It is through making just such distinctions that we understand the world, insofar as we *do* understand it. It is, furthermore, through the ability to make such distinctions that we *devise* the world after having evoked its possibilities in language. The man who cannot make such distinctions is not merely a fool, he is a dangerous fool. Should we put him in charge of *any* of our processes, or even in charge of the preludes to their onsets, he will botch the work. If we're lucky his botch won't kill us or cause World War III, but then again we may not be that lucky.

That provost has been given not an education but a handout of material. His rudimentary language evokes, as language always does, an unseen world, but it is a cloudy and uncertain one. If he were running a hot-dog stand on the corner, that wouldn't be so bad, but he is a high-ranking officer of what we call an educational institution. In that position, he pretends to have knowledge and technique. If we don't listen to him carefully, he may well fool us into believing that he does have those things, and we will suffer him to devise for others the same kind of education that has made him what he is. Succeeding generations will see the geometrical multiplication of people whose thinking ability is such that they will nod wisely at the mention of a prelude to the onset of a process consisting of components, elements, and factors. When we have enough of these people, the lunatics will take over the management of the asylum.

They may have already done so. Do you suppose that that provost is the only high-ranking academic official in America whose thinking is clouded by bad language? Anyone who snoops around in the academic world can assure you that he is typical of the people who make important policy in all our schools. It is perfectly true that many of the worst of the jargon-mongers seem to be remote from the schools — sociologists and psychologists and bureaucrats and businessmen of all kinds, for instance. Nevertheless, they all come from the schools. In every measurable way, education is the largest of our social institutions; hardly a single citizen escapes its influence. The propensity for jargon and bad language is a sickness not of this or that calling but of thought itself. The main business of education is to teach the process of thought and the operation of the symbol systems in which we think — language and number. When education fails to teach thinking, it fails in everything, and everybody talks nonsense. Since the schools infect everybody, it is not possible to discover a calling whose effectiveness has not been diminished by the sickness of thought and language that are spread in the schools.

Here, for instance, are the words of a forester, a healthy, red-blooded American who loves, no doubt, the woods and streams and the brisk smell of the balsam. He is describing a part of his work, the selection of attractive campsites:

> The method is based evaluating two basic groupings the authors [he's working with an accomplice] feel are vital in considering where campgrounds might best be located. Those groupings, physical and socio-economic, are broken down into sub-headings which in turn are expanded into lists of sub-variables. The idea was to have trained observers visit pre-determined potential campsites and rate them according to a set numerical rating system, supposedly reflecting degree of campground excellance. Priorities in campsite development were the product of the socio-economic data. When the two ratings were combined a list of prioritized campgrounds and their existing physical status would result, and hopefully provide the planner with a feeling of confidence as the next step was taken.

Try to ignore the small errors in grammar and spelling and the awkwardness of the prose. Remember Natty Bumppo, who spoke wisdom even though his subjects and verbs didn't always agree. We have to allow woodsmen a little latitude. Ask yourself rather just what, exactly, is this woodsman up to when he breaks physical and socio-economic groupings down into subheadings and then expands those subheadings into lists of subvariables. Ask also what it means to call the groupings "vital" and how we could possibly expect anyone to visit some *un*predetermined potential campsite. Forget your uneasiness about "hopefully" — it doesn't matter — but ask what is meant by the "existing physical status" of a campground and how it could possibly "result." Then ask where and how this doughty woodsman came to suffer such brain damage. It didn't happen in the woods; it happened in school.

The jargon that is handed out in the schools harmonizes all too happily with their moral and metaphysical pretensions, which are best expressed in the vaguest possible terms. While vague, however, the terms must sound important and must leave the impression that if you and I don't understand them clearly, it is because we are laymen to whom these mysteries have not been opened. The language of jargon arises from ignorance, but, once constituted, establishes itself not as *knowledge*, of course, since that would invite verification, but as wisdom, a matter presumably of the heart and not the reason. Our schools have become the temples of a mystery religion, and their graduates, from provosts to foresters, have at least learned the lingo of the rituals.

# 10

# Grant Us,
# O Lord

One of the most important uses of language in all cultures is the performance of magic. Since language deals easily with invisible worlds, it's natural that it provide whatever access we think we have to the world of the spirits. Even in cultures that overtly deny a belief in the spirit world, the anthropologist from Mars would discover in their language evidence that denies the denial. The Jiukiukwe address elaborate incantations to the Great-grandfather Anaconda just as the Manhassetites exhort their cars to start and the stock market to rise. Wherever language exists, it is used in the attempt to constrain, or appease, or flatter, or beseech the spirit world.

Typically, the language of incantation is oblique and arcane, always distinguished in some formal way from the language of everyday speech. The gods and spirits are ordinarily not addressed by name, unless you really have their numbers and can *command* them, and the benefits sought are usually phrased in delicate euphemisms and contrived circumlocutions. There are also, in all languages, certain magical words, words not common in the daily lexicon and sometimes known only to the initiated few. If you know these words, you can at least compel the attention of the spirits. For any speaker of a language, its use displays his license of membership in the culture and elicits from other members whatever is included in the list of privileges and benefits, but a more special form of the language can admit him to inner circles. The most special forms of all are understood to admit him into the spirit world itself. It is not uncommon that the priestly caste of a culture goes even beyond a special form of the language and adopts, if only for ceremonial purposes, an entirely different language.

We have no more confidence in the priests, but that is by no means to say that we have no more confidence in magic. We have simply consecrated new priests to its service. We cannot, in fact, abandon magic, because our language *assumes* the existence of persons and powers not of this world, the world of immediate experience, and if among them we can perceive "mankind" and "gravity," we can also perceive such things as "Lady Luck" and "fate." These entities are not *in* the corporeal world; they dwell in language. They can be evoked and, in some sense, dealt with, through language, provided, of course, that we know exactly what to say. The assumption of a spiritual reality underlies "Bright star, would I were steadfast as thou art" as well as "Rain, rain, go away." It is the root of poetry. It is also the root of lots of gibberish — the abracadabras and open sesames of our time.

The new priests are rarely found in churches. They flourish everywhere. Wherever some inner circle of initiates undertakes to deal in arcane formulae with the insubstantial, there must be a priesthood. It will have all of the gimmicks and trappings of any other priesthood. The candidate for consecration will have to undergo lengthy training in lore and ceremony and much study of the holy writings and will, at the last step, have to satisfy the adepts that he is worthy to sit in their company. Once admitted, he will be granted powers and privileges, among them the power of a highly specialized form of language and the privilege of being taken seriously by the multitudes when he utters it, however little meaning they may take from what he says.

Many of these priests are professors. They have learned their lore and lingo in our colleges and universities, and there they lurk. Sometimes, to be sure, some of them go into classrooms to practice the skills of Delphic utterance and to look for the occasional promising novice whose calling can be confirmed through *his* aptitude for Delphic utterance, but mostly they spend their time in untroubled meditation and earnest prayer. To them we turn for the fruits of their meditation and prayer. What, we ask, is the meaning of it all? How can we know the good? How will it fare with us in the future? Their answers are prompt and lengthy, but unintelligible. They meditate, you see, on inputs and parameters, on teaching situations, learning situations, passing situations, and even on situation situations, and on things like general insight into the knowledge of a discipline. And for the answers to those universal questions that vex us, they pray not to some god for favor but to some grant for funds.

In the whole United States of America at this moment there are only twenty-seven college professors who have not at one time or another sat around with a few accomplices and plotted to think up a good gimmick for a government grant, *and* the wording of the prayer that would bring the money. (A grant from some foundation is even better; those G-men are fussy about little things like bookkeeping and expense accounts.) Grant-getting has become one of the regular duties of some professors and administrators. Many colleges and universities have established whole bureaucracies devoted to grant-getting, and energetic hustlers, who never forget, like the rest of us, that Barnum was right, go from campus to campus offering, at stiff prices, seminars, workshops, conferences, and revival meetings on the art of the successful grant prayer.

The enterprises supported by these grants often reach some interesting conclusions, or "findings," as the priests call them. They frequently discover some truth on the order of: Cornered animals will fight. Orphans, they reveal, don't get enough attention from their parents. It has been definitively demonstrated at public expense in New Jersey, for instance, that students who are learning to write learn better the more they write. That's not all. The same "studies have shown" that teachers of writing teach better in those rare cases when they themselves can write. Those conclusions may have cost a lot of money, but they're worth it, wouldn't you say? Knowledge is power.

The search for a grant usually begins with an impromptu worship service also known as brainstorming or as a bull session. The term "brain storm" was coined in 1906 by Harry Thaw's lawyer. Clouds of witnesses had seen his client pumping bullets into Stanford White, so it seemed that the defendant would need something more than an alibi that would place him in a bowling alley in Union City that very evening. Accordingly, the cunning advocate convinced the jury that Thaw had suffered, that very evening, a violent fit of passing madness, a brain storm, which momentarily excused him from certain moral imperatives. Thus Thaw escaped the electric chair. We must presume, therefore, that there is no point in taking what would seem the appropriate action with regard to the concoctors of grant proposals. It would probably be impossible to get a conviction.

Brainstorming sessions go something like this: Some professors are dawdling over coffee in the faculty dining room. They are complaining about the quality of the students these days, the difficulty of finding parking spaces immediately adjacent to the buildings in which they teach occasionally, the stupidity of the dean, and the difficulty of promotion. One of them adds that he can't stand to teach in room 322 because the blackboard is at the back of the room behind the students, and when he wants to draw some cabalistic symbols, he has to thread his way through the desks. In another age, this wouldn't have been all that bad, but nowadays the girls are wearing denim workshirts buttoned up to the neck. Someone suggests moving the furniture around, but this is ignored as not worthy of an academic discussion. Why not, someone else asks, just stay there and lecture at their backs? Maybe the students would learn more because they wouldn't have to pretend to be attentive, and besides, it's easier to check your zipper. By now things are getting serious.

The bright young radical, an assistant professor who used to have a beard when he was only an instructor, points out that the traditional arrangement of a classroom is militaristic, even fascistic, and therefore unsuitable for a nonauthoritarian education in a democratic society. Wouldn't it be interesting to see what would happen if *all* classes were taught from behind? That does it, of course, and someone says the words, the incantatory formula that opens to the faithful visions of a new, and better, much better, world: "I bet you could get a grant."

Even right after a big lunch, college professors are hungry. Someone says, Hey, why don't we write it up? What can we lose? A little time, that's all. Time is something college professors can find lots of, and we can easily imagine the document that might come of the idle rapping: "A Proposal to Study Pedagogical/Instructional Outcomes as Related to the Unconscious Symbolism of Traditional and Non-Traditional Placement of Individual Learning Stations within the Primary Learning-Facility Location . . ." Of course, that's just a rough draft.

That language is necessary. No project officer would look twice at the naked truth. "What would happen" must become "Pedagogical/Instructional Outcomes," and it would be even better if "behaviors" could be fitted in somehow. (If you speak of "behavior" in the singular, your degree is revoked and you are sent to do penance by teaching in a ghetto school in Tulsa. You may, however, speak freely of "a behavior.") "Placement" seems insufficiently modified. There's no such thing as too much modification, and "Placement" has only the meager "Traditional and Non-Traditional." After all, anyone who knows what he's talking about has to prove it by making it clear that by "placement" he means putting something somewhere in a place, and that place is in space, right? Right! Let's have "Spatial Placement." Come to think of it, "Proposal" is standing there naked — it has no modifier at all. How about "Tentative"? God, no! We'll never get a grant with anything tentative. Maybe "Research Proposal"? Not bad. Or even "experimental." I mean, it *is* an experiment, after all. Even better. Why not take both? "An Experimental Research Proposal." That should do it. Someone murmurs, How about "theoretical/

experimental"? and although that's obviously a good idea, it's too late. The phrase has already been jotted down in big, black capital letters.

Someone now suggests "subliminal" in place of, or even in conjunction with, maybe with a slash, "unconscious," but nobody else likes it. It sounds too Madison Avenue, and it might take some of the bite out of "Unconscious." "Unconscious" is a very potent word — it's something psychological, Freud, you know, and it's very "in" these days. On with the work. Desks have been handled very nicely with "Individual Learning Stations," but it won't hurt at all to change that to "Individualized Learning Stations." Everyone is delighted with "Primary Learning-Facility Location" for classroom, and the hard part is done. We now have the proposal in what is ritually known as its "finalized" form:

An Experimental Research Proposal to Study Pedagogical/Instructional Outcomes/Behaviors as Related to the Unconscious Symbolism of Traditional and Non-Traditional Spatial Placement of Individualized Learning Stations within the Primary Learning-Facility Location

Of course, it still needs some work, now that we see it in its finalized form. "Study" is puny and insufficiently affective. After all, we're not just going to study something; who'd pay us for that? We have to be more positive. Let's try "evaluate"; everybody is willing to pay big for "values" these days. Even "to evaluate," however, seems a little pale. We'll probably end up with "to critically evaluate" or perhaps "to critically/objectively evaluate." That has the power of the slash and shows that we're not stodgy about infinitives.

That just about does it. All that remains is to cook up

a few corroborative details, stuff like the instruments (that means tests), the controls, the hypotheses, the expected findings/outcomes, and the questions that the study/evaluation will be centered around. (These things are invariably described as "centered around" something. That is, of course, a metaphysical proposition understood by the priests, but a mystery to us laymen.) Now we can shoot the whole thing off to HEW or someplace, and with a little bit of luck and the favor of the hidden powers we'll all be on half time for the next two years. That means longer lunches and more brainstorming, and, who knows, why not, maybe we can even think up another grant.

Historically, priests have never troubled to deny that their language had the effect of concealing secret things from the uninitiated but revealing those things to the adept. Nor did they feel any need to deny it, since those were goals thought legitimate by both parties, who were in agreement that in language was the key to open doors into other worlds, but that to use it required some special and difficult mastery. Ancient priests, however, seem to have used their special mastery of language to talk about (and even *to*) things that they at least believed to be real, although impalpable, and inexpressible in any other way. The brainstorming grant-seekers, on the other hand, know very well that a desk is real and palpable and easy to express and *therefore* choose to veil it as an Individualized Learning Station, thus suggesting mystery where they know there is none. Where the ancient priests spoke in such terms as they could devise of things not to be understood in the ordinary vernacular, the modern priest speaks of things easily understood in language *not* easily understood. The mystery has migrated from the thing itself to the language. Under the circumstances, in this age of disbelief, they've done the best they could.

They have the words, but they just don't have the tune. Where the language of magic was once the visible shell of the unimaginable within, all that is unimaginable now is the shell, because what is within is obvious and prosaic. The modern priests have no substantial core, not even an imagined one, to put at the heart of the arcane language of incantation and prayer.

Consider this passage from a grant-seeking proposal meant to do something or other about the training of teachers:

(1) Teaching is the application of a *systematic series of actions directed toward specific ends*. [Italics in original.] (2) Within the general system of teaching acts are many subsets of actions and processes. (3) For example, based upon developments in philosophy, psychology, and communications theory, teaching and learning are now seen as reciprocal relations within a specialized system of information processing. (4) Teaching also requires the ability to relate knowledge of the processes of human growth and psycho-social development to the instruction of individuals and groups. (5) Translation, transformation, and organization of subject matter into meanings appropriate for the age or ability of learners is another process within teaching.

Knowledge is a collection of statements. Not all our statements, however, are statements of knowledge. Language wouldn't work if it didn't have abiding forms and structures, but sometimes it doesn't work just *because* it has those forms and structures. We're free to put anything we like into the natural forms, and, because the forms *are* natural, it's easy to conclude that we have said something because we have said it in the same form in which we might *in fact* have said something. Since it makes some sense to say "lions are dangerous," we may think that any other statement in that same form will make some other sense. This form, however, is so brief and clear that not many of us would be confused into thinking that "lions are ultimate" has to mean something just because of its form. When both form and matter are more complicated, it's easier to be confused.

Remember the questionnaire. Take the perfectly reasonable statement, "A goal of teaching is to give students knowledge." Not especially startling, or even useful, it is at least a statement that can be accepted as meaning something. It is an empirical hypothesis that could imaginably be checked through observation and experience. Its form, however, is a container into which we can pour whatever we please. We can say, as that silly questionnaire did say, "A goal of teaching is to provide general insight into the knowledge of a discipline." It sounds fine; but if you bother to think about it, you see that it is nonsense. Of course, you're not expected to think about it; you're expected to *feel* about it.

When you solicit the favor of the hidden powers with prayer, you do not presume to instruct them in matters intellectual. It is not your wish that they *understand* what you say, but that they *love* you for saying it. Consider the first sentence in the passage quoted above: "Teaching is the application of a *systematic series of actions directed toward specific ends.*" It is grammatically impeccable. It sounds just like a meaningful statement. It *is* meaningful. It, too, is an empirical hypothesis that we might conceivably confirm or confute through experience and observation. It has, furthermore, the sound of authority, with all those careful modifiers and distinctions. Can't you just see some gray, distinguished professorial gent, tweed and pipe, pushing his glasses up on his forehead, staring awhile in deep thought at the book-lined wall of his study, and revealing at last, you hanging on his every word, not only that teaching is a systematic series of actions but that it is actually directed toward specific ends? Those words are even put in italics, which means that this is the heart of the matter, and you'd better pay attention if you want to learn something.

That, as it happens, was a mistake. In the cool calm of the book-lined study you might be sucked into believing that you had been told something important, but when you can consider the words on paper, and in italics at that, you can see that this is a statement designed to leave a certain impression on those who pay no attention. That was the case, also, with that business about providing general insight into the knowledge of a discipline.

When we pay attention, we can see that the statement, while certainly reasonable, is simply worthless to anyone who does in fact want to understand teaching. It purports to tell us what teaching is and tells us what just about anything is. Take the name of whatever it is you do for a living, or, for that matter, as a hobby, and drop it into that form in the place of "teaching." It'll make sense. It will still be rubbish. But not, of course, worthless rubbish. Grant-seeking, after all, is also a systematic series of actions directed toward specific ends.

The second sentence has the same characteristic; it can describe anything we do: "Within the general system of teaching acts are many subsets of actions and processes." It is cunning, however, because it sounds as though the writer has thought something out and is now elaborating on the first sentence. He will be delighted if you nod your head and say, "Oh, yes. Now I understand. Subsets. Sure. Subsets of actions and of processes."

That sentence is a perfect example of the Principle of Unnecessary Specification. It's the sort of thing that's often found in the language of incantation, where it sometimes has poetic and impressive qualities: "We have erred and strayed . . . we have followed too much the devices and desires of our own hearts." In such appearances, the elaboration of specification, probably an inheritance from certain typical forms of Hebrew poetry, often does provide delicate distinctions interesting to think about. In the modern priest-jargon, however, this is seldom the case. When we are told that a "general system" is made up of "subsets of actions and processes," our minds are not notably clarified.

Usually, in fact, such examples of the Principle of Unnecessary Specification are meant to be the opposite of clarifying. Indeed, its practitioners are traditionally careful not only to provide detailed specification where none is needed but also to withhold it where it *is* needed. What, for instance, are those presumed "developments in philosophy, psychology, and communications theory"? Furthermore, where specifications are provided, they are either obvious, as in the case of the subsets of actions and processes, or incomprehensible, like the miniature incantation in the fifth sentence: "Translation, transformation, and organization." A solemn sound. In some metaphysical fashion, the three are one in the mind of the writer, obviously, because when they finally get a verb toward the end of the sentence, it's the singular "is." "Translation, transformation, and organization . . . is another process within teaching." Who says faith is dead? This triune mystery is made up of lesser mysteries: The translation of subject matter into meanings, The transformation of subject matter into meanings, and The organization of subject matter into meanings. Quite a trick. That's not all. If they mean what they say, we have to conclude that the "meaning" of Magna Carta suitable for stupid nine-year-olds just wouldn't do for normal high school seniors.

Let's try to understand all of this. First of all, this writer seems to allow that there is such a thing as "subject matter." This is a handsome admission from an educationist, but it is not, of course, an endorsement of the foolish notion that subject matter is what is to be taught. The teacher, we see, has to take the subject matter and "translate" it into "meanings" appropriate for these or those students. If you're sitting there wondering what it might mean, for instance, to translate the formula for finding the area of a circle into "meanings" more appropriate for some students than for others, then you're just not thinking. For students in the Italian quarter, you talk about pizzas; for students in Dubuque, apple pie; in Laredo, tortillas. That's only the beginning. Now that the subject matter has been translated, it must also be transformed into, presumably, yet other meanings than those derived by translating it. And then organized. That part sounds simple at first, because we *can* imagine ways of organizing subject matter, while it passes understanding to see how we can translate or transform it. However, although we might organize subject matter in any number of ways, that won't be good enough. . . . Somehow, we must be sure that our organization converts the subject matter into "meanings" precisely appropriate for exactly these students.

The ordinary citizen in the streets imagines that teaching geometry, for example, must be a fairly straightforward business, at least in principle. You show the students the assumptions and explain the principles; you demonstrate the methods; you provide problems and guide their practice; you go logically from step to step, and the students can learn not only geometry but skills and discipline useful for thinking in general. Wrong. For professionals of education, if we are to believe this document (and you had better believe it), the geometry itself is only the humblest first entry in a hierarchical structure of acts and subsets of actions and processes and reciprocal relations within a specialized system of information processing and the *relation* of knowledge to the processes of human growth *and* psycho-social development *to* the instruction of individuals *and* groups. There. Then there's the business of translating geometry into those appropriate meanings, and transforming it ditto, and organizing it ditto. Now you can understand why the teacher of geometry in your local high school may be a little weak in the geometry itself and why that unfortunate girl in Pennsylvania can't punctuate. They have spent most of their time in college not actually studying things like geometry and punctuation. They have been occupied with the solemn contemplation of all the subsets of actions and processes, in all of which they were "taught" by gurus to whom naked geometry and mere punctuation, of which they may well have known nothing at all, were nothing more than convenient starting places for an exercise in transcendental elaboration. The study of education isn't like the study of plants or history; it's like the study of angels.

You must not be curt when you address the hidden powers. They have all the time in the world, and you must come before them as one who is properly initiated into their ways. To address a prayer to the grant-giver, you must show that you have what a court of law would call "standing." That's why the Principle of Unnecessary Specification is so important. Anyone who would confess, for instance, that he is concerned with mere "instruction" cannot expect much of a hearing from the grant-giver. That's why this document is careful to explain that it is interested in the "instruction of individuals and groups." You and I would think it enough to say "instruction" and understand that there isn't anyone else to instruct except people, who come to be instructed either as individuals or groups, because there isn't any other possibility. Obviously, the grant-givers, either as individuals or groups, do not need to be instructed as to this; they must want to know the nature of our hearts, or something. The pious heart, you can be sure, would have gone on beyond "individuals and groups" if only some further category had been imaginable. The writer was probably a bit saddened to have to say such a meager thing, and it may have been to make up for it that he devised the sonorous "translation, transformation, and organization" formula for the next sentence.

The Principle of Unnecessary Specification is, of course, a great convenience for writers who need to pad out what little they have to say, and it is certainly true that many a grant proposal has been rejected out of hand because it wasn't long enough, but padding isn't the only purpose of that splendid principle. It has genuinely incantatory intentions and powers. It can make the obvious seem profound, and the simple, complicated. It can, furthermore, make the trivial seem very important indeed. Skillfully used, it projects an atmosphere, one might even say an aroma, of great insight and expertise about anything we might write. It is the incense of incantatory prose, and a few deep whiffs can transport the intoxicated worshiper into what grant-seekers of all persuasions would surely call "new levels of awareness." When we ascend to those new levels, we do so not in elevators, but in "integrated single-module vertical transportation systems," as they are in fact called in government documents, and the mentor who elevates us must be an "integrated single-module vertical transportation system operations engineer."

This may be silly language, but it is not the ignorant language of that schoolteacher in Pennsylvania. It is carefully and knowingly contrived. In fact, the constraints that must be observed in this language are even greater than those laid upon the priests and necromancers of earlier ages. They had to satisfy only the hidden powers and, occasionally, each other. These modern spell-casters must always be mindful of pesky and impertinent outsiders who nowadays presume to poke their noses into all sorts of things too deep for them. The very taxpayers and parents of schoolchildren have come to think that they have some right to understand — and even to question — the intentions of the rulers and the clergy, the professionals, as they call themselves. It's exasperating, but lacking a general return to the social beliefs and standards of an earlier and easier time, there isn't a hell of a lot to be done about it. Nevertheless, although they can't send an uppity laity back into the Dark Ages, they can at least find a way to keep it in the dark. Their language must serve the double purpose of showing the hidden powers that they deserve the dough and making the ordinary layman believe that what they think about is terribly complicated and important, too complicated for him to understand and too important for him to meddle with.

In this respect, the passage cited above is not entirely successful. We *can* understand it, with a little attention, and we *can* see that what little it says is so general and obvious that it's not worth saying and that most of it says nothing that means anything at all. The writer, of course, would still object that mere laymen cannot understand such technical and esoteric things, but his objection would carry little conviction. We've caught him in just too much nonsense. He is not a truly great writer of balderdash, just a hack.

He misses greatness because, not having read Luther, he sins but meagerly. His transgression is puny because while his heart is in the world of noncognition, he wants to sound cognitive, like some of his respectable colleagues who still deal with discernible facts. He doesn't mind *living* in Cloud-Cuckoo-Land, but he and his close neighbors have made a pact among themselves not to give out their addresses. In short, he is willing to utter nonsense, but he is afraid to be caught doing it, so he has to sound analytical and "official."

Like love, however, perfect inanity casteth out fear. The next writer has not only moved into the land of noncognition but has even taken up arms in its perpetual war of worldwide conquest.

# 11

# Spirits from the Vasty Deep

Bad writing is like any other form of crime; most of it is unimaginative and tiresomely predictable. The professor of education seeking a grant and the neighborhood lout looking for a score simply go and do as their predecessors have done. The one litanizes about carefully unspecified developments in philosophy, psychology, and communications theory, and the other sticks up the candy store. The analogy is not perfect, of course, for the average lout seldom nets more than thirty-five dollars per stickup, and he even runs some little risk of getting caught. Nevertheless, the writing and the stickup are equally routine and boring. It's not often that we find ourselves admiring these criminals, therefore. Once in a while, however, some unusually creative caper pleases us with its novelty or its audacity. So, too, with the works of the grant-seekers, perhaps because creative force is so much less common in grant-seekers than in other culprits.

We turn now to just such an enterprise. If it were only a little bit less illiterate, it would seem to have been written by someone who had read deeply in Luther and even Nietzsche and had decided to sin boldly and to hell with *Sklavenmoral*. We find here none of that meager, mealymouthed obsequiousness that piously assures us that teaching and learning have now been shown — *really* — to have something to do with one another. That's the tepid prayer of a half-baked scholastic. What follows is the work of a veritable academic dervish:

Project WEY — Washington Environmental Yard (1972) is a manifestation of the intercommunal, process-oriented, interage, interdisciplinary type of change vehicle toward an environmental ethic from the school-village level to a pan-perspective. The urban focus of the project as the medium has been inestimably vital since it is generally speaking the message. Situated near the central downtown area of the city of Berkeley and a mere block from civic center, Washington Elementary School courts the thousands of daily onlookers/passersby (20,000 autos!) traveling on a busy boulevard with easy access to the physical transformation and social inter-actions (at a distance to close-up) — a virtual open space laboratory. It has served evocatively as a catalyst for values confrontation, even through a soft mode of visual/physical data exchange system. Since 1971, the dramatic changes have represented a process tool for the development of environmental/educational value encounters on-site/off-site, indoors/outdoors and numerous other bipolar entities and dyads. The clients represent a mirror of the macro-world just as the children and parents of the school reflect more than thirty different ethnic groups — as one of numerous dimensions of diversity.

It is difficult to comment on this writing, and dangerous as well, since too much attention to this sort of thing may well overthrow the mind. The earlier passage is at least decipherable, but this is a form of contemporary glossolalia and not to be grasped by the reason alone. It requires the gift of faith as well.

We do see, at least, what it's all about. It's about a change vehicle, of course, a change vehicle toward an ethic. We know also that the focus has been vital, inestimably vital, in fact, so we need not expect that there will be any attempt to estimate the degree of the focus's vitality. That's good. We don't know for sure, of course, but we can reasonably guess, since the school courts all those onlookers/passersby in their 20,000 autos when they ought to be paying attention to their driving, that the busy boulevard is probably strewn with tangled wreckage and the dead and bleeding bodies of motorists. The carnage, apparently, serves as a virtual open-space laboratory of social interactions resulting in physical transformations. What could be clearer?

We know that some "it" or other — the school? the project? — has itself served, and evocatively at that, as a catalyst for values confrontation, "even" through a soft mode, which makes it clear that it is unusual for something to serve evocatively as a catalyst through a soft mode, but that *this* something has nevertheless managed to do so and thus deserves generous funding. We see that changes have somehow *represented* a tool, a tool for the development of all sorts of doubled-up things, including certain unspecified but surely numerous and important "bipolar entities and dyads." (Here we must be careful not to commit some sacrilege; bipolar entities might be some kind of powerful spirits, and those dyads might be something like those dynamite chicks that lurk in trees.) And, just as changes have represented a tool, the clients have represented a mirror. There. That gives us a process-oriented pan-perspective.

The writer of this interesting passage, just one paragraph of a grant proposal, is paid by taxpayers to teach would-be teachers how to go out into the world and make comfortable livings being paid by taxpayers as teachers of something that is called Environmental Education. Environmental Education, along with its numerous cousins, deserves some attention, not because it is interesting or important in itself, but because it is, or perhaps it *represents*, a triumph of language over intelligence. All the cousins do the same. They are things like Health Education, Consumer Education, Intercultural Education, Sex Education, Career Education — the tribe is too numerous to list in full. Besides, new progeny are spawned every semester.

These educations are the Snopeses of education itself. They are aggressive and determined and trashy enough not to be subject to the scrupulous restraints of the genteel tradition. The meek, betweeded professors of philosophy must surely succumb some day to something that will probably be called Values Education. Intercultural Education, for instance, has already seized the high ground once held, but diffidently, by the anthropologists, and it will be a vigorous and profitable industry when anthropology has become a quaint, antiquarian specialty like Sanskrit. Consumer Education starts with what used to be a single lesson in seventh-grade arithmetic — how to write a check, remember? — picks up a little substance from the budgeting lesson in home economics, and goes on to displace economics itself along with a good hunk of sociology and biology — preparing nutritious meals, you know. (In fact, home economics and sociology had it coming; they were Snopeses in their time.) Flem Snopes started out by boosting himself a piece of a little diner on the outskirts of town and ended up owning the bank and most of the real estate. His numerous relations followed him in geometrical proportions. We can expect that each of these educations will draw others in its train and birth hosts of new educations.

This metastasis of educations is only in part a social phenomenon; it is also a linguistic phenomenon. The power of language is so great that it can call things into existence simply through naming them. At this moment, for instance, there is no such thing as enharmonic interpersonal dynamism, but all it needs to become the subject of a profitable self-betterment book or even a whole new subject of study in the colleges is an energetic go-getter who can write it up. There will be converts and workshops. There will be scholarly papers and appearances on talk shows. Dissensions and heresies will arise, and the neo-enharmonic interpersonal dynamists will contend with the revisionist enharmonic inter*cultural* dynamists. Money will be made, and swarms of the addlepated will most unexpectedly make livings. Some of them will buy whole wardrobes of polyester double-knit leisure suits and become professors of Enharmonic (now we can give it capitals) Interpersonal Dynamism Education. Although we will pay the cost in dollars, the empire will be built of words.

Obviously, if Enharmonic Interpersonal Dynamism (EID, okay?) is to get off the drawing board, one of the first things it will need is a grant. If we can show how EID can provide an inestimably vital change vehicle toward the reciprocal relationships of teaching and learning suggested by the latest findings in philosophy, psychology, and communications theory, we can easily convince some saps in the federal government to fork over the funds. It's a little more complicated than sticking up the candy store, of course, but the potential profit is larger, inestimably larger, in fact. Furthermore, if you get caught sticking up the candy store, many rough people will treat you rudely. If you invent EID and make it famous, you'll be offered tenure at the teacher's college of your choice.

Such things actually happen. Consider the example of something called Career Education. The Jiukiukwe have no word for Career Education, nor could they, for their language does not permit the modification of one noun by another. (It is no accident that some of our greatest follies flow from the fact that we can string nouns together with abandon.) Of course, the Jiukiukwe have only the one career, banging trees with stones; even fish-finding is so rare that they think of it more as an avocation. They would be baffled, naturally, by the term Career Education. We are baffled, too, but we have to pretend not to be lest we be taken for elitist reactionaries. How then, we must figure out, do we come to have, and at considerable expense, something called Career Education, which is *not*, as the innocent might think, a training in the necessary skills of this or that career?

Unlike the Jiukiukwe, we have many careers, and there are still some American schoolchildren who think that they would like to grow up and make an honest living in one of them. It used to be that a mere education in reading and writing and ciphering was thought a good beginning for just about any career. As certain careers became matters of greater and greater technical skills, it began to appear that the would-be nuclear physicist or neuro-surgeon might do well to start some of his training as early as possible. This is obviously not an inane idea, but it also *isn't* the idea behind Career Education. The practitioners of Career Education can hardly have such a concern in mind when they arrange for third graders to visit the bagel factory and study the work of the head bagel-baker. What they have in mind is the presumed necessity of revealing to the children that there *is* such a person as a bagel-baker so that peace and harmony and tolerance will break out among us. That's not all. Maybe some of those darling kiddies would like to become bagel-bakers themselves. And why not? It's an honorable trade. So here are some clever tests (instruments) designed to discover bagel-baking aptitudes even in third graders. There are brigades of people who make, and score, and interpret such tests, and other brigades who then sit down and take counsel with the third graders about their chosen careers as bagel-bakers. And *that's* not all. How can a third grader choose a career without profound self-knowledge and some insight into the value system inherent in the various careers? We need to offer courses that teach these things to third graders, and yet other courses to teach the teaching of these things to yet larger children who can then find career satisfaction and fulfillment as teachers of Career Education. This sort of thing, as most of you will remember, used to be taken care of by an occasional captioned picture in the reading book: "The policeman is your friend. He helps you cross the street and takes you home if you are lost." That's about as much as any third grader needs to know about a career in law enforcement.

So what would *you* do if you had to fill a handful of pages on the subject of Career Education? What else *is* there to do? You simply must string a whole lot of words together. All of that stuff — and more, much more, whole books full — is a perfectly inevitable consequence of the simple existence of the term Career Education. You might play the same game for yourself by inventing your own education. Somebody has probably already taken Media Education and Commuter Education, but you might try things like Recreation Education and Religion Education. It's important that both words be nouns. Notice that Religion Education is different from Religious Education, for instance. Religious Education might actually have some subject matter; Religion Education, however, would be aimed not at teaching this or that *about* a religion but at alerting students to the fact that this or that religion does exist and suggesting how they might want to feel about that. In like fashion, Investment Education, a likely candidate, would not undertake to teach people how to invest. It would reveal that there is such a thing as investing and that it makes America strong.

The process obviously has no limits, because our language has no limits. Anything we can talk about, we can talk about. Consequently, we can expect that by this time next year there will be at least three schools in which the study of history has been replaced by highly relevant rap sessions called History Education. Courses in History Education will not bother students with the terms of the Treaty of Versailles or the details of the growth of American Federalism. They will provide the students with a personal appreciation of the fact that there *is* such a thing as history and that we are *all* a part of it — isn't that wonderful? — and that even the least of us is, therefore, relevant. Literature Education and Mathematics Education are still in the planning, or preproposal, stages, but their day will come. And just wait till you see Foreign Language Education, which will raise students' consciousnesses about the many marvelous languages spoken all around the world by all sorts of people whose very interesting value systems we really ought to appreciate as much as we can. After all, there's no real or relevant need to learn the language of the Jiukiukwe. Let's learn to appreciate what the nature of that language tells us about those simple but warm and wonderful people whose treatment of their senior citizens ought to be a lesson to us all.

All of the "educations" are strings of words, of course, not things in the world. Once we have the strings of words, however, we can go about and do things in the world so that some part of it may come to look like the thing we have described in the words. There's nothing wrong with that; in fact, there's everything right with that. That's how ideas and the institutions they generate come to be in the first place. It is in strings of words that we make ideas. The words, however, can say anything that the language permits, which, in our case, is quite a lot, so a string of words can just as easily express inanities as ideas. When inanities *are* expressed, we can discover them just by paying attention to the words.

Here are the words in which our mystical prophet of Environmental Education expresses the aims of his chosen career:

A topian educational system of values and its existing isomorphic, formulated goals and means can be traumatically challenged by EE (Environmental Education) and its evolving, diverse-goal system as EE functions as a catalytical non-discipline to prepare and facilitate people to move through a meta-transition into the phase of non-stationary culture . . .

A catalytical non-discipline. We can understand what a non-discipline is like just by considering the word "topian." It might refer to those Pompeian wall decorations called "topia," but then again it might not. Perhaps it's supposed to be the opposite of "utopian," but also maybe not. Perhaps a topian system is a system that actually *is* someplace, in a *topos*, and is thus characterized to distinguish it from the "evolving, diverse-goal system," which is, presumably, *not* someplace. If you find yourself traumatically challenged by these choices, that's good. Pick whichever you please. In a non-discipline it doesn't matter. That's why non-disciplines are so rewarding to teach — you can't get anything wrong. Be grateful that you have been facilitated to move through a meta-transition into a phase.

It would be a polite euphemism to call the writer of that barbarous nonsense an illiterate. The word just doesn't do the job. The writer, however, is a university professor supported by taxpayers. He has degrees in education, and has satisfied others of that clan that he is worthy to sit in their company. What did they ask of him? How did they decide that he was, indeed, worthy to profess? Was it his vast knowledge of his subject? Obviously not; his "subject" is a non-discipline. Was it his power to communicate the nonexistent knowledge of his non-discipline? Well, yes. In a *way*, yes, that is. It must have been his power to sound as though he might well *be* communicating some unknowledge in a non-discipline. They must have thought that he could, indeed, call spirits from the vasty deep. His prose, like the thinking it reveals, is full of cloudy suggestions of something beyond the range of mere cognition. He has been given power, if not over the entities and dyads, certainly over the ignorant and superstitious. Who else would sign up for courses in a catalytical non-discipline?

Both grant-prayer examples evoke images of a world that is not, of course, and in that way they are alike. In each case the image is the image of the mental world where the writer dwells, whether he knows it or not. The worlds are different, however, because this priesthood, like any other, has its conservative wing and its lunatic fringe, its Thomists and its Pentecostalists. The first writer (back in chapter 10) is orthodox and self-satisfied. He evokes a world in which pale abstractions move among the spheres in cycles and epicycles, or subsets of actions and processes. Translation, transformation, and organization, elemental, immaterial entities, merge and fuse into the transubstantiation of "meaning." This is a world untouched by human hands. In the universe of "education," no grubby brats bedevil harried teachers; no chalk dust clouds the air; no trays clatter to the floor in noisy cafeterias; no smelly socks litter the locker room. We find only fleshless principalities and powers, developments and relations, developments in philosophy, psychology, and communications theory, reciprocal relations and abilities to relate. This is a world where any minor German metaphysician of the nineteenth century would feel right at home, but where Walt Whitman would run lunatic.

Strangely, people who write and think like that insist that they are champions of what they have named "humanistic" education. They think, or they say that they think, that education ought to instill certain socially desirable attitudes and humanitarian values, and, accordingly, that a teacher must be "humanistic." A teacher who is too knowledgeable in his subject is likely to become a "mere" expert, a slave of information, so the humanistic educationists take care to prevent that by arranging that would-be teachers spend as little time as possible in the study of any subject. This gives them more time to spend in humanistic studies where they can develop abilities to relate. But the language gives the game away. That grant-writer simply isn't interested in anything human. Indeed, he isn't even interested in anything concrete. He is interested in spirits.

The Environmental Educationist, on the other hand, is a visionary of apocalyptic enthusiasm. In his world a focus speaks a message and a manifestation of a vehicle toward an ethic materializes, or almost, out of the swirling fogs of off-site/on-site indoors/outdoors bipolar entities and dyads. He opens the seventy-seventh seal, and a catalytical non-discipline facilitates us to move through a meta-transition into a phase. In miraculous fashion, not to be understood by reason unaided by revelation, clients "represent" a mirror, and changes, a tool. It's *Walpurgisnacht* in a soft mode of a visual/physical data exchange system. Where the first writer is a would-be theologian pretending to reason, the second is a shaman pretending to dance up demons. And he does, he does.

Our shamans may be false, but they have danced up real demons. As we have become more and more aware of what is happening in education and language — they go together — we have sought remedies. The shamans have promised us cures. The cures are all lethal.

# 12

# Darkling
# Plain English

We have all been charmed and gratified in recent times by what seems to be an official attempt to stamp out jargon and gobbledygook. From a President himself we have heard a call for plain English, and state legislatures here and there are drafting and passing laws requiring simplicity in the wording of contracts and regulations. We are delighted to see that lawyers and moneylenders, also landlords and insurance companies, are opposed to the process. Anything that displeases those odious enemies of clarity and good sense must be desirable, and the cause of plain English is beginning to attract not only politicians who see in it a safe way to please the public but many of those good-hearted citizens who used to be members of SANE.

Here is an example of the sort of thing that infuriates the advocates of plain English. It's an extract from one of those handbooks put out by the Occupational Safety and Health Administration, an outfit notorious not only for its torture of English but for the fact that many of its thousands of rules and regulations render each other what they call in Washington "inoperative." It's hard to decide whether the people at OSHA are simply ineffectual bumblers or supremely talented satirists boring from within. Here, for instance, is how they define an exit: "That portion of a means of egress which is separated from all other spaces of the building or structure by construction or equipment as required in this subpart to provide a protected way of travel to the exit discharge." That's not all. Now they elaborate on "means of egress": "A continuous and unobstructed way of exit travel from any point in a building or structure to a public way [which] consists of three separate and distinct parts: the way of exit access, the exit, and the way of exit discharge."

That's certainly ugly, and it makes us wonder whether an exit has to be defined at all, and, if it does, why couldn't it just be called a way to get out. Then we wonder why a "means of egress" has to be defined at all, and, if it does, why couldn't it be called a way to get to the exit. If these reservations seem reasonable to you, it's because you're just not thinking. You are assuming that any ghastly mess of verbiage that comes from a bureaucracy needs to be simplified because it is needlessly complicated to begin with. Wrong. As it happens, that horrid prose serves its aims perfectly. Regulations of this nature have one clear purpose, and that is to answer, before the fact, any imaginable questions that might be asked in a court of law. For that purpose it's not enough to assume that everyone knows what an exit is. Is a door an exit? Maybe, but maybe not, if a drill press just happens to be standing in front of it. Is a hole in the wall acceptable as an exit? Do you really get out of the building (let's say it's ready to blow up) if you go through a door and find yourself in an enclosed courtyard instead of a "public way"? You don't have to be very clever to think of lots of other such questions, and the writer of this regulation is thinking about your questions. He has done a good job, although he has written something very ugly. But it's *only* ugly; it's not wrong, it's not more complicated than it has to be. It doesn't need simplification; it needs simply to be kept pretty much out of sight, lest it provide some plain English fanatics with what they think is a useful example.

There are, of course, lots of things that ought to be written in such English as the citizens may understand, but there are lots of citizens who ought to learn to read the English in which it is necessary to say some things. This is not a distinction that the plain English faddist is always able to make. For many of them, though, it doesn't really matter.

The marvelous thing about the plain English fad, for a politician, is that there's no way it can hurt him. If he fights for automobile safety or for gun control, he's bound to lose some votes and some campaign contributions. On the other hand, if he comes out against automobile safety and against gun control, he's bound to lose some votes and some campaign contributions. Politicians have to balance things like this all the time, always hoping to make a little more on the peanuts than they have to lose on the popcorn. It's not easy, and they're delighted, actually, whenever they can find a cause with a high yield of profit and very little overhead. Plain English is just such a cause.

True, there are a few opponents of the simplification of legal and public language, but just look at them — a pack of notorious scoundrels. You can always show a profit when you castigate lawyers, moneylenders, and landlords. Not only are these enemies of good sense unpopular, but their case against plain English is difficult to present and difficult to understand, and, coming from them, sounds suspiciously self-serving. The case for plain English, on the other hand, is so easy to state and seems so reasonable that it now ranks with those splendid self-evident truths so dear to all Americans.

How can we tell whether or not something is written in plain English? It's simple. We have a couple of systems available that call for counting words and syllables in the average sentence and dividing something by something or maybe multiplying something by something after we have divided something by something. And there you have it — a rational, concrete index in the form of a number, a plain English score. A "good" score means, naturally, that lots of Americans can understand it, and a "bad" score means that few Americans can understand it. Theoretically it ought to be possible to write in such a way that *no* Americans can understand your English, or so that *all* Americans can understand your English. In fact, the former is common, but when we find it we rarely discover that its difficulty has anything to do with sentence length or numbers of words and syllables. The latter, however, is impossible, since there are so many Americans who can read nothing at all. Those various indexing systems are not meant to deal with the extremes. They want only to say, of this or that piece of prose, that it probably calls for an eighth-grade ability to read, or a college graduate's ability to read, or something like that. Let's hope that the scale is adjusted year by year, since this year's eighth graders, like this year's college graduates, don't read quite as well as last year's, although they do read a bit better than next year's. Unless the indexers give this some thought, we'll be faced with a continual downward revision of all those laws and contracts and regulations, because this year's newly revised and simplified driver's license application form that almost any high school graduate can read will be, in 1994, incomprehensible to those who hold master's degrees in sociology or doctorates in education.

The problem has some entertaining qualities. We have found ways to produce every year more and more high school graduates who can barely read. More and more of the citizens are finding, accordingly, that more and more documents are hard to read. The automatic populists, now common among us, see an obvious solution to this problem. If the people are having trouble understanding what is written, then we must write it more simply. It's analogous to the view that if the people haven't got the brains to buckle their seat belts or to refrain from sticking their hands into the blades of their lawn mowers, then we must redesign the seat belts and the lawn mowers. We reveal thus that our national commitment to education is pious hypocrisy. If we really believed that the people could be taught, we would teach them the worth of buckling their seat belts and keeping their hands out of the lawn mower blades. We would even teach them to read, not just enough to puzzle out some slightly complicated prose, but to read, when necessary, the inevitably complicated expression of complicated ideas. It's as though you went to the hospital with a broken arm and the people in the emergency room, instead of setting the thing, got busy on the telephone trying to find you some other line of work, something that requires only one arm.

Like all cockeyed social notions, the plain English movement invites us to look around and see who's going to make a profit from it. A paranoid observer might think to detect a massive conspiracy. And here's how it goes:

First we start providing the schools with lots of taxpayers money to support research into quaint and curious innovations in teaching children how to read. This results in some extraordinary gimmick, and a very profitable one, not only for some professionals of education who are paid to cook it up but especially for that massive educational-industrial complex that makes and sells at high prices books and flash cards and sets of gadgets to go with every new fad. These people, of course, would like to see as many new fads as possible, because each one makes all the old stuff obsolete. What the gimmick is, is not important; for a while, and in some schools still, it was the weird notion that reading would be better taught without reference to the sounds of letters but rather through identifying whole words as symbols of something. The latest gimmick seems to be speed reading, which will make it possible, at a stiff price, to read a complete gothic romance in three minutes and forty seconds, thus ensuring a steady market for gothic romances. A well-trained keypunch operator could go through sixteen of them on her lunch hour, provided of course that she ate something like a sandwich or a slice of pizza. Speed reading does require the use of at least one hand.

Let the gimmick be whatever it is. Think of your own, if you need an example, something like printing vowels in different colors or providing new and tricky shapes for certain letters. These, of course, have been done, so you'll have to stretch a bit; and, when you do come up with something that seems unspeakably zany, keep your mouth shut. If you mention it in public, it won't be long before someone offers to fund it. It's best to avoid offering the occasion for sin. But enough. Let's say we have a gimmick.

Now we experiment, being careful to use methods and controls that would make a first-year chemistry student blush and stating the problems and the expected results (those we call "outcomes") in the silliest possible jargon. Don't worry, we'll "prove" the efficacy of our gimmick (remember the new math?). As a result, or outcome, although we'd rather not use that word in the singular, more and more students in the public schools will read less and less.

Do not make the mistake of thinking that this means that our gimmick has failed. Pay attention. This means that the gimmick has succeeded. Remember, we have taken the role of dentists handing out lollipops to ensure that there will be no falling off of customers. Now that things are worse than ever, we view with alarm the "reading problem" in the schools. It's time for a new round of grants, projects, experimental proposals, expensive consultants, packets of materials, instruction booklets, sets of visual aids, more teachers, carpeted classrooms, air conditioning, just about anything you can imagine. It's all good for the education business, and if it seems to have been exaggerated, just you go footing around yourself and find anybody anywhere who proposes that we can teach reading (or anything else) better by spending less money.

If there were a conspiracy that worked all these wonders, you can imagine the joy of the conspirators in the windfall that the plain English agitation has brought them. In one way it's a happy result of that conspiracy, and perhaps, therefore, not unexpected. Naturally, as fewer and fewer literate people move out of the schools and start signing leases and borrowing money for Corvettes and stereo systems, it more and more appears that the documents put before them are just too hard. They're always too hard for somebody; it's just that now we have more and more of those somebodies, and the problem grows more visible. It becomes a cause; it suddenly seems that we can make a case for rudimentary English as one of an American's inalienable rights. You deprive him of that — it's practically like forbidding the sale of classic comics or those benoveled versions of movies. It's a splendid cause for politicians and educationists, especially, because anyone who opposes it must do so either out of some devious special interest by which he lives or out of a positively un-American elitism intended to maintain a rigid class structure and deprive the ignorant of access to professorships in philosophy and literature. Both politicians and educationists will profit from the cause, the politicians at once, in good will and support from the public, and the educationists somewhat later, in more grants, and because they will sooner or later be the very ones called on to do the necessary simplifying.

The bureaucrats who have produced most of our dismal official English will, at first, be instructed to fix it. They will try, but *nihil ex nihilo*. That English is the mess it is because they did it in the first place and they'll never be able to fix it. They write that kind of stuff because that is the kind of stuff that they write. Ultimately, in desperation, they will call on those people who say they know about these things — the professionals of reading and writing. There will be lucrative jobs and consultancies available in every branch and department of government for remedial-reading teachers. The foxes will be made the guardians of the hen house.

Here is an example of what the bureaucrats will do when left to their own devices. The following passage is from a document called "Draft Regulations to Implement the National Environmental Policy Act." It *has* been rewritten into what they call plain English, and a covering letter from the chairman of the President's Council on Environmental Quality says that it "represents an extraordinary improvement over the existing guide-lines":

> The agency need make the finding of no significant impact available for public review for thirty days before the agency makes its final determination whether to prepare an environmental impact statement and before the action may begin only in one of the following limited circumstances: . . .

Remember, this has been simplified; the original is hard to imagine. There are no difficult words in this passage — even the five syllables of "determination" do not make it a difficult word, whatever they might do to the passage's score. What these people *mean* by "determination" might be better served by "judgment" or even "decision," but still, most readers will not be baffled by "determination." In fact, there's nothing at all — neither word nor thought — nothing at all difficult for any moderately educated reader in that passage. Why then is it so hard to understand? Why do you have to read it over a couple of times, should you really care to know what it means? Does this passage, already simplified from God knows what, need further simplification? No. All it needs is a little attention to the stuff that used to be taught to sixth-grade students back in the days when sixth-grade students actually wrote compositions.

People who have learned even a little about how English works have all heard about modifiers. They know that a modifier is something that tells us something about something, and that there are many kinds of modifiers, some with tricky names. The way we teach things like this, as though they were subject to arbitrary rules like the rules of basketball, is so stupid and tedious that most people block out modifiers as soon as possible. The English system of modification, however, does not exist in a set of paltry rules that do what they can, and fail, to describe some very elaborate operations not simply of the language but of the mind. To say that an adjective modifies a noun is worth nothing unless we see that sticking adjectives on nouns is the outward equivalent of some mysterious inward process that goes on in the mind. It's not entirely absurd to think that somewhere in the past of mankind someone, for the first time, did in his mind the equivalent of putting an adjective to a noun, and saw, not only a relationship, but *this* special relationship between two things of different kinds. That moment was more important to our history than the flight of the Wright brothers. In sum, all the seemingly complicated kinds of modification in English are just ways of thinking and seeing how things go with each other or reflect each other. Modifiers in our language are not *aids* to understanding relationships; they are *the ways* to understand relationships. A mistake in this matter either comes from or causes a clouded mind. Usually it's both.

This passage clouds our minds not because what it means to say is difficult, not because the matter is too technical for most of us, but for a very simple reason. In effect, it says that the agency need do something only under certain circumstances. That's a clear thought. They need do A only when B. The nature of the relationship between A and B is tucked into the words "need . . . only." In the passage, thirty-four words intervene between "need" and "only," so that by the time we see "only" we have forgotten to expect any further modification of "need." It's like finding one more step when you thought you had reached the landing. Between those two words, furthermore, we may have been a bit bewildered by something that sounds like a modification but isn't: "impact available for public review." It takes a moment to look back and see that "available for public review" is actually supposed to go with "finding." When we add to those two failures — failures of the writing to match the modification systems of the mind — the tedious parade of words and clauses not yet related to any idea that we can identify, the passage becomes what it is, awkward, puzzling, and exasperating. It requires of us more attention and backtracking than its ideas are worth.

This passage does not need simplification or even a change in its choice of words. It needs merely to have been written by someone with elementary skills in finding the right thing to do on the page to call forth certain things in the mind. The idea is not complicated; the prose, in fact, is not complicated — it's just bad. Nevertheless, it *could* be simplified even using that vocabulary. Here's how it might go:

> In some cases, a finding of no significant impact *does* have to be made available for public review. Public review means that you have to give the public thirty days to look it over before you can even decide whether to write an environmental impact statement, and certainly before any action is taken. Here are the cases in which you do have to provide the public review:

There. All we need now is to draw little pictures.

The people who write like this write like this simply because they are the people who write like this. Even when you can convince them that there is something wrong with what they have written, you cannot make them into people who wouldn't write like this. If you send them to go and fix it, you'll get what you deserve — it's like hoping the termites will build you a new house out of the glop they have made of your old one.

So the bureaucrats will need help, and lo, help is at hand. The educational establishment that has provided the problem will come forward to be paid for the solution. Thus firefighters sometimes set fires so that they can try out the new pumper. Hosts of advisers and consultants will be added to bureaucracies of all kinds. New courses of study will appear in the schools to prepare people for such lucrative and respectable labors. New courses of study will appear in the teacher-training academies to prepare the teachers for the teaching of new courses of study that will prepare the advisers and consultants. New journals of the new study will blossom; new workshops and conferences will convene from Tacoma to Key West; new federal grants will support studies that will find new findings. If you had any sense at all, you'd buy some stock right now.

There is, of course, an alternative to the plain English fad, but it's almost too dangerous to discuss in public. We could simply decide to educate all Americans to such a degree that they could read and understand even the OSHA definition of an exit. We could even educate them well enough so that they could understand why OSHA has to say things like that and why it doesn't matter much. We could have the schools devote lots of time, especially in the early grades, to spelling and vocabulary and even writing so that the next generation will grow up able to grasp relative clauses and complex sentences at sight and understand at once the meaning of "reciprocal" and "indemnify" and even "mitigate." This sounds so easy and so right that there must be a catch, and indeed there is. When we consider the inevitable consequences of such a policy, we can see that it is probably too dangerous to contemplate.

Just think what happens in the mind of the person who knows the difference between restrictive and nonrestrictive clauses. Anyone who understands that distinction is on the brink of seeing the difference between simple fact and elaborative detail and may well begin to make judgments about the logic of such relationships. He may start bothering his head about the difference between things essential and things accidental, a disorder that often leads to the discovery of tautologies. Furthermore, anyone who sees the difference between restrictive and nonrestrictive clauses is likely to understand *why* modifiers should be close to the things they modify and thus begin to develop a sense of the way in which ideas grow from one another. From that, it's not a long way to detecting non sequiturs and unstated premises and even false analogies.

Unfortunately, we just don't know how to teach skillful reading and writing without developing many undesirable and socially destructive side effects. Should we raise up a generation of literate Americans, very little of the America that we know would survive. We depend on a steady background level of ignorance and stupidity. A skillful reader, for instance, cannot be depended upon to buy this after-shave rather than some other because he is always weighing and considering statements that just weren't meant to be weighed and considered. He may capriciously and irresponsibly switch not only from one after-shave to another but even from one hot comb to another. Our industries depend on what we call "brand loyalty," and thoughtful readers will all be brand traitors. They may, even probably will, go the next step and become brand nihilists who decide not to buy any after-shave or hot comb at all. It may even occur to them that the arguments for the ownership of trash compacters and toaster ovens are specious, and then they won't buy any trash compacters or toaster ovens. Economic chaos will follow.

The next thing you know they'll start listening very carefully to the words and sentences of the politicians, and they'll decide that there isn't one of them worth voting for anywhere on the ballot. There's no knowing where this will end. The day will come when a President is elected only because those few feebleminded citizens who still vote just happened to bump up against his lever more often than they bumped up against the other guy's lever. A President, of course, doesn't care how he gets elected, but he might lose clout among world leaders when they remind him that he owes his high office to the random twitchings of thirty-seven imbeciles. That will be the end of network election coverage as we know it.

# 13

## Hydra

Unfortunately, the plain English movement is probably not the result of a widespread conspiracy. That's just wishful thinking. It's simply one more head of the many-headed monster of muddled language and thought. If there were a conspiracy, it might conceivably be thwarted, but if we cut off the plain English head, another will grow in its place, and perhaps a more horrid one.

At one time I thought that I was the victim of a conspiracy myself. I was certain that the Admissions Office had salted my classes with carefully selected students, students who had no native tongue. Many of my students seem unable to express themselves in any language whatsoever. They aren't utterly mute, of course. They can say something about the weather and give instructions about how to get to the post office. They are able to recite numerous slogans, especially from television commercials and the lyrics of popular songs and recent — very recent

— political campaigns. They are able to read traffic signs and many billboards and even some newspapers, and they can claim certain emotions with regard to various teams and even individual athletes, whose names they often know. They can spin more or less predictable reveries about the past or the future either in very simple concrete terms or in sentimental banalities, or both. But they cannot pursue a process; they cannot say why evidence leads to a conclusion; they cannot find examples for analogies. They've never heard of analogies. They speak and write English as though they were recent immigrants from Bulgaria, whose Bulgarian itself had been totally obliterated on Ellis Island.

Of course, it was all an illusion, a phantom of wishful thinking. There was no conspiracy at all. They were just ordinary American students pretty much like any others. They were the typical product of our schools.

Everyone who has succeeded in learning a foreign language has come to "think" in that language, as we say, although we probably mean something even more complicated than that. Now it seems that there are millions of Americans who can't think even in English. How is it with them? Do they plan, or do they merely fantasize? Do they solve problems, or do they simply rummage around for a suitable slogan? Are they the people Socrates had in mind in thinking about that unexamined life that wasn't worth living? Can they examine life?

People in that condition don't think of themselves as being in that condition because they don't *think* of themselves — they don't think at all. To think, we must devise connected chains of predications, which, in turn, require fluency in language. Those who are fluent in no language just don't have the means for thinking about things. They may remember and recite whatever predications experience provides them, but they cannot manipulate them and derive new ones. Mostly, therefore, they will think and do those things that the world suggests that they think and do. For some of us, it must be very important that people in this condition remain in this condition, for we have obviously devised ways to see to that.

Truncheons are for louts. The great masters of social manipulation use language. They know, furthermore, that the establishment of a flexible and subtle language for the ruling classes is only half of what's needed. The other half is the perpetuation of an ineffective and minimal language among the subjects. Ordinarily, the second half is assured by man's natural propensity to bother himself as little as possible, but history occasionally requires that the rulers take some special pains to preserve the ignorance of their subjects. Our own recent history provides a splendid example of how this is done.

The civil rights struggles of the early sixties made it look, for a while, as though the public schools might, in fact, become integrated someday. That turned out to be an illusion, of course, but in those days it did seem possible that millions and millions of poor black children would find themselves in "better" schools, schools where white children (we thought) were being taught the skills suitable to *their* place in society. In those days we took out some insurance so that social disorders might be averted.

America depends on the poor black population of its cities to be always the same. They are a reactionary's dream, an utterly stable segment of society. Every year, without fail, they will consume just so much junk, just so many TV dinners, and just so many pay-by-the-week burial-expense insurance policies. They will invest a predictable proportion of what little they have in lottery tickets and patent medicines. They will keep the whole legal system employed by committing, quite regularly, an ever-growing number of crimes, mostly against each other, fortunately. Some few of them will always provide a never-failing pool of utterly unskilled labor to do the necessary scut-work that underlies the technology that the rest of us can handle. They will support prodigiously the enormous illegal drug industry and contribute vast sums to all those along the line who profit from it, very few of whom are to be seen in the streets of the ghettos. They will buy couches and lamps and refrigerators of the sleaziest quality on the never-never plan at fantastic rates of interest. There is simply no counting the benefits they bestow on the rest of us.

It is a foolish oversimplification to think of poor blacks as wards of the state supported by the taxes of the middle class. They don't eat that money. They spend it. It all comes back to *some* of us with interest. Millions of us have good jobs because of the poor. Millions of us have good jobs because of criminals and junkies. What would come to pass with us should we wake up one morning and discover that all the black poor had vanished in the night? What would America be like? Whatever else we can say about such an America, we can surely assert that it wouldn't be like *this*.

Imagine now an event less drastic and by no means impossible, however unlikely. Imagine that next June should bring us a million — that's all, just *one* million — black high school graduates who could speak and write clear, correct, fluent English. Andrew Young and Barbara Jordan we can handle — sure — but a million? That would be the end of affirmative action as we know it.

A fluent command of English cannot exist as an isolated skill, a clever stunt. A person who speaks and writes his native tongue clearly and precisely does so because of many other abilities, and those other abilities themselves grow stronger through the fluent manipulation of language. The simple matter of being logical is a function of language. A million high school graduates capable of fluent English would be a million Americans capable of logical thought. What would we do with them, especially if they were black? You think *they're* going to buy those lottery tickets and lamps in the shape of Porky Pig? You think they're going to hang out on the corners and provide employment for everybody from the local social worker to the justices of the Supreme Court?

Well, don't worry. It's just a bad dream. Next June won't even saddle us with a million *white* high school graduates who are fluent in English. That too would be trouble.

Even hypothetical trouble is worth worrying about, however, and in the sixties the possibility that black children would become literate someday was at least hypothetical, and, therefore, dangerous. Some unknown genius somewhere came up with an effective vaccine against black literacy. He contrived a gimmick that would certainly postpone black literacy for decades and perhaps forever. Like all truly great inventions, it was simple and obvious, once we saw it, of course. It was Black English.

To understand how the schools could have embraced something as silly as Black English, it is necessary to understand something about the people in those schools. Many of them drifted into teaching because of a disquieting and usually well-founded suspicion that their talents would not permit them to find much success as accountants or insurance adjusters. As compensation for meager ability, they discovered in themselves an abiding love for children, however horrid or grubby. Some of them found, once in the classroom, that their love for children was even greater than they had thought, and *they* became administrators as quickly as possible so that they might ladle out that love to whole *schools* full of children, even to whole school *systems* full of children. In the schools, rank and honor are accorded to the lovers of children inversely in proportion to the numbers of children with whom they deal. Those who deal with many children every day have the lowest rank. Those who deal with only a few from time to time have higher rank — and pay. Those who never have any reason at all even to *see* a child from a distance are general officers, usually dignified with the title of "educators."

All of these people, of whatever rank, rule over children, and some of them rule over some rulers of children. It is a calling that must cause, sooner or later, serious self-doubt in all but the most cloddish. That's why people in the schools will seize with fervor any novelty in pedagogy. There's no way to measure the effectiveness of a teacher who undertakes to teach what cannot be measured. If you put yourself forth as a teacher of arithmetic, you might be embarrassed when it turns out that your students can't do arithmetic, but when you claim to be teaching Positive Self-Image — who's to say? Black English is even safer than Positive Self-Image, for it doesn't have to be taught at all, merely applauded, and the teachers who applaud it automatically earn merit as teachers of Positive Self-Image and even of Intercultural Understanding. Accordingly, Black English, a concept just about as sensible as Black Arithmetic or Black Botany, swept over the schools like the impis of Chaka.

We were all feeling guilty in those days, anyway, and Black English seemed to offer us an opportunity to make up for past inequities and transgressions. Perfectly sane professors and even deans could be seen going around the campus in hair dashikis and saying "right on" to each other. It was suddenly revealed to us all that subject-verb agreement was an instrument of imperialist oppression, and we were deeply ashamed of having expected it of *any* of our students, whatever their color. We were about to institute courses in Swahili, but somebody discovered that Swahili grammar requires that the speaker know how to make careful distinctions in the form and placement of object and subject pronouns and even requires subject-verb agreement. It turned out to be just another instrument if imperialist oppression, and that was the end of Swahili. Besides, it was a foreign import, and we were all talking about the right to a language of one's own.

Like any argot, Black English can be eloquent and poetic. While it is not in any sense at all a different *language* from English, it is in social terms at least what Old English once was to Norman French, the private talk of the oppressed. It is rich in subtle invective. It provides vast arrays of synonyms in a few very special subjects, most notably money, sex, and the enemy. Its extravagant lexicon seems the result partly of a desire to exclude outsiders and partly of the exuberance of skillful performance. In the mouth of a fluent speaker it is a powerful incantation. It is, furthermore, an illustration of the many differences between speech and writing, as anyone who tries to write discursive prose in Black English will soon discover.

It is only a sentimental populism that can pronounce Black English a "language" just as rich and useful as standard Anglo-American or any other tongue. Had Freud been thinking about language when he told us that the goose dreams of corn, he would have said also that the goose *speaks* of corn.

Eskimos have many words for different kinds of snow, just as the Jiukiukwe have many words for different kinds of tree-bangers. This is, however, obviously due more to environment than to the nature of their languages. Should the Eskimos run amok and conquer the world, the time would soon come when only the oldest grandparents remembered all of that vocabulary. Such special vocabularies are ordinarily related to matters of intense, even vital, interest. They can make exceedingly fine distinctions that may, in fact, mean the difference between killing a fat seal and freezing to death. In like fashion, although not often against the threat of death, our language offers large, specialized vocabularies, so that we can assemble whole dictionaries of terms used in medicine or philosophy or even insurance adjusting.

We think, at first, that Black English, or any argot, shows the same linguistic complexity, but it doesn't. Like slang anywhere and in any language, for instance, Black English provides countless words and expressions with sexual meanings. Here, too, we might assemble whole dictionaries. If we did, though, we would discover that many of those words, in fact *most* of those words, mean exactly the same thing. If you want to explore this phenomenon without disconcerting yourself too much, think of money instead of sex. You'll quickly assemble a splendid array of synonyms, but that's all they are — synonyms. They are not specialized terms intended to make finer and finer distinctions among various possible *kinds* of money. Such vocabularies, furthermore, are always ephemeral, and if a dictionary of slang is useful, it's useful not because it reveals fine distinctions but because it explains the bawdy jokes in Shakespeare. If the snow lexicon of the Eskimos were altered every twenty years or so, they'd die.

The extensive, specialized vocabularies of slang are clearly not intended to describe the world of experience more and more precisely. They are, rather, exuberant outpourings of the joys of word-play, colorful elaborations perfectly proper to speech and poetry. That's why slang, and especially what we call Black English, can be so jaunty and rambunctious and pleasing to the ear. Its metaphors can be subtle and penetrating, and its blithe disregard of standard grammatical forms is as crafty as it is cocky. Unfortunately, however, it will not serve us when we want to explain or understand the rationalistic epistemology that informs constitutional democracy or how birds fly. A child who comes out of school knowing only Black English will never trouble us by seeking employment as a professor of political science or as an aerodynamic engineer.

Here are the unacknowledged assumptions behind the Black English movement in the schools: Most black kids are too stupid to learn fluent, standard English. Some few are, perhaps, not too stupid, but to teach them fluent, standard English is hard work for the teachers. (Some of the teachers are too stupid to teach fluent, standard English, anyway.) It would be better, in any case, if they *didn't* learn fluent, standard English, since we would then have to admit some of them to important and lucrative professions. Black parents can be calmed into approving this scheme through appeals to "ethnic pride," which we will also "teach" in the schools just to provide a little extra insurance. We can explain that spelling and punctuation are devices of racial and economic oppression and that verb forms that change in the past tense are the result of centuries of prejudice and intolerance. They'll buy it.

And they did. They still do. Although we don't talk

about it much anymore, the Black English mania has not gone away. It has even been reinforced with Bilingual Education, another mania with many similar unspoken assumptions. When we look around the country and see that schoolchildren are more ignorant than ever, and that black schoolchildren are ordinarily the most ignorant, we are inclined to think that something has failed. That is a naive conclusion. In fact, something has succeeded.

# 14

# The Turkeys
# that Lay
# the Golden Eggs

Consider P. (That's not his real name, of course; his real name is Legion.) He is a member of the most elaborate and successful bureaucracy since the days of the Austro-Hungarian Empire. Is there a Kafka hidden away in one of its back offices? Maybe, but he surely isn't P. P's prose is somewhat less interesting than K's, although it does have one unusual quality that Kafka never managed to achieve. While Kafka *can* be translated into English, P cannot:

> Our program is designed to enhance the concept of an open-ended learning program with emphasis on a continuum of multi-ethnic, academically enriched learning using the identified intellectually gifted child as the agent or director of his own learning. Major emphasis is on cross-graded, multi-ethnic learning with the main objective being to learn respect for the uniqueness of a person.

Blot out all thought of trying to figure out what he means — it doesn't matter. Concentrate on P as a *person,* or even as the uniqueness of a person.

We already know a lot about P, because we have seen similar productions turned out by many of his ilk. He is one of those educationist types, no longer a teacher, if he ever was one, but a permanent bureaucrat, one whose love of children has excused him from their *presence* as persons so that he may respect their uniquenesses as persons. We can be sure that he knows and uses, perhaps even thinks that he understands, all the typical jargon of his calling. We can guess that he has taken many courses in pedagogy and academic administration and that he knows all about guidelines and curricula and what the studies have shown. His writing suggests also certain personal qualities. It is pompous and self-important, intended to impress the reader with the skill and erudition of the writer. Most of it, moreover, seems to be taken from "the literature," that is, the utterances and pronouncements of all the other P's. Because we can't tell if there is any thought in what he says, we obviously can't tell if there is any *original* thought in what he says, and we can only guess that there probably isn't. Let's guess that, by all means. All right — that's enough. We have a fairly good picture of P.

Now ask: Is P unusual? That seems unlikely. We find so many examples of P-ness, especially in the administrators of the schools, that we have to guess that there are many like P, hordes of them, in fact. They are the people who sit around sending each other pieces of prose like the one above. They take them seriously. They are the people in charge of education. Politicians come and go, but these educationistic bureaucrats are permanently bedded down in secure bureaucracies and protected from criticism by the opacity of their words and their claim to an expertise that you and I cannot possibly hope to understand. They will make the future.

Go back now to politicians, more P's, come to think of it. Although politicians do come and go, they are able to do much mischief during their brief tenure. As you saw in that business of "simplified" English, politicians especially love issues that can't possibly hurt them. Nowadays, they have discovered the turkeys that lay the golden eggs in our educational disorders. Because few people can read anything much more complicated than the instructions on the child-proof caps, the politicians can without risk espouse the cause of simplification. For the same reason, that is, because it is without risk, they can advocate improved teaching of reading in the schools.

If we really believed that the reading of schoolchildren could be improved, then we wouldn't need to worry about simplifying all our contracts and regulations, of course. But to politicians a little contradiction like that doesn't matter. What matters is that they take a stand in favor of good and against evil. Accordingly, in state after state, legislators are making laws intended to ensure what is now called a minimum competence in all high school graduates. It's a popular cause, and many reasonable people have been tricked into supporting it. Only a yahoo would attack it, it seems. Nevertheless, it is a very bad idea for the future of literacy, and, when combined with the simplification madness, it assures a never-failing supply of docile voters and mindless consumers. It assures also, like the Black English mania, that the technological skills of the future will be concentrated in the hands of fewer and fewer people. For those people, that's good.

Here's how the process goes. Politicians begin to notice that the citizens have been worked up about declining literacy. After asking around, they discover that there's hardly anyone who will come out *against* literacy, so they decide to do the virtuous thing however difficult and politically dangerous. They say: Enough! Our high schools must prepare every citizen and voter to cope with the world. No more social promotion! No more functional illiterates! Freedom of opportunity for all! And the people applaud.

What next? Tests, of course. We will give tests to those students, and those who can't pass can't graduate. What could be more logical? And how will we make those tests? We'll go to the professionals, the educators, the people who have been sending all of those illiterates out into the world, the people who caused this problem in the first place. They have by now surely mended their ways; even they have come out in favor of literacy. It's a great new day for education and freedom and politics in general.

Here is what happens down at the bitter end of the process. Don't forget P, the chap who wrote that stuff about the cross-graded multi-ethnic learning. He and his friends are the ones who will figure out how to measure literacy. Who else is there to do it? The legislators are a little short on literacy themselves, and P and company have all kinds of certificates and diplomas, to say nothing of a well-established bureaucracy and the secret lodge language. They are the people to whom the legislators turn. P and his pals will "devise instruments" to guarantee minimal competence in reading and writing in all high school graduates.

As horrifying as that is in theory, it's much worse in practice. It means that P will end up giving tests in which literacy is measured by a student's ability to choose between "who" and "whom" and to put a colon after "Dear

Congressman:" Now *that* is the kind of stuff that P knows how to measure. *He* probably does know the difference between "who" and "whom," and very probably can even say, after only a moment's reflection, hard things like "just between him and us." Judging from the passage cited, we may even conclude that he has some control of commas and understands at least one use of capitalization. If those are the kinds of things that constitute literacy, however, then it's hardly worth fussing about. Knowing those things obviously hasn't helped P at all. If we really mean to stamp out illiteracy, then we're going to have to start by stamping out P.

Indubitably, the literate person is familiar with the conventions of "correct" English and can use them or even fool around with them as he chooses. Knowing the difference between "who" and "whom" is like knowing how to finger scales; the one doesn't make you literate and the other doesn't make you a musician. The writer who *doesn't* know the difference between "who" and "whom," like the musician who doesn't know how to finger scales, had better have one hell of a lot of talent. There are such people. They are amazing, but they are not produced by schooling. Such people, in fact, ought to stay away from schools and protect their talents. The ordinary student has little if any talent, and if he is to become literate he will need to know all the mechanical trivia we can teach him. That, however, will not make him literate.

The literate person is in control of those techniques special to writing rather than to speech. He can formulate sentences that make sense. He can choose the right word from an array of similar words. He can devise the structures that show how things and statements about things are related to one another. He can generate strings of sentences that develop logically related thoughts, and arrange them in such a way as to make that logic clear to others. He can make analogies and define classes. He can, in writing, discover thought and make knowledge. Because he can do these things, he can, in reading, determine whether or not someone else can do these things. He is familiar with a technology of thinking. To accept anything less as our definition of literacy is to admit that hardly any of us will ever be able to think about anything. That may be true, but to admit it is to assure it.

P is illiterate. He cannot do those things. Wait. Maybe he *can* do those things but for some reasons of his own chooses not to. In that case, he is worse than illiterate; he is depraved. Let's give him the benefit of the doubt and say that he is *merely* illiterate. When we realize that, we also realize that "minimum" is the important word in the "minimum competence" game. P is going to set some standards having to do with things like "who" and "whom." He'll call them, naturally, behavioral objectives. He'll devise some instruments to measure the behaviors. The teachers will teach the students the "who" and "whom" business, along with colons, maybe. The students will take the tests. A number of them, perhaps lots of them, will "pass." Behold. A minimum competence in literacy will have been achieved. Legislators and educationists will shake each other by the hand. The former will be reelected; the latter will be promoted. The citizenry of America will be enriched by millions of high school graduates who now know the difference between "who" and "whom."

The minimum competence school of education is nothing new. We've had it for many years, but we didn't talk about it until we discovered that we could make a virtue of it. Obviously, any system of schooling in which there are tests and passing grades is a sort of minimum competence system — if you pass, you pass; but that's not exactly how the minimum competence system is now construed. Now we try to find out just how little we can get by with and pronounce it enough. The current crisis is simply the result of a disagreement as to how little is enough. The school people want it to be as little as possible, and the politicians want it to be just enough to convince the citizens that something *has* been done, and somewhere in the middle they will meet and compromise. In some states now it is enough if high school seniors can read and write like the eighth graders of another age, but in other more demanding states it is necessary for high school seniors to read and write like the tenth graders of another age. States' rights, you know.

In effect, the minimum competence movement will simply assure that millions of American students will take just a little longer to reach that degree of incompetence that we can now expect in the ordinary high school graduate. This, in turn, will mean that it will take just a little bit longer for millions of American students to reach that degree of incompetence that we can now expect in the ordinary college graduate. This, in its turn, will keep graduates of both high schools and colleges out of the job market a bit longer. Unemployment will decline because those who might have looked for work are still busy wrestling with "who" and "whom." Educationists will point with pride to their new "rigorous" programs, and politicians will point with pride to the efficaciousness of their economical policies. America will prosper.

That's not all. The educationist establishment will wax fat with the addition of diagnosticians and remediationalists and devisers of instruments and coordinators of curricula and directors of programs and all of the supporting services and paraphernalia that must go with all of those things. The teacher corps will grow, and teachers will demand and get more money for the arduous increased labor involved in teaching the advanced skills of fourth-grade reading and writing to sixth-grade students. Everyone will profit. Well, perhaps not everyone.

Here is someone who won't. This poor fellow went to high school not too long ago. Then, even more recently, he went to college. His major was political science, his minor, sociology. In his major, his grade average was B plus, in his minor, B. These grades used to mean a better than average student; now they mean an average student, except, of course, in education courses, where such low grades are uncommon. This poor chap's name is also Legion. He's your standard model college graduate. Now he needs a job, and here he is, applying for a modest enough position in the world of free, private enterprise:

Dear Sir:

I am seeking a job as an insurance adjuster; and it is with this in mind that I am writing to you and your company. I first became interested in an insurance adjuster job through my best friend. He is an insurance adjuster with a large national company. After having talked to him I have decided that an insurance adjuster job is the type of job and career that I would enjoy. I sought placement with the company that he works for, however at this time they were unable to find placement for me with their company; and as I am very interested in becoming an insurance adjuster I have decided to seek placement with other insurance companies. My first approach to trying to find placement with other insurance companies was to go to a personnel agency which had listed several adjuster positions that they had. However after having visited a personnel agency I decided that they were not the best approach in trying to find placement with other insurance companies. Therefore, my second approach and the one that I am using now is to send a letter with my personal resume to all the insurance companies operating in the state of North Carolina, stating that I am seeking placement with their company as an insurance adjuster. After you have read my letter and studied my personal resume, if you and your company have an opening within your company for an insurance adjuster and are interested in me as a candidate for the position, I would be very interested in talking to you.

What will become of him? Do you think that he can make it as an insurance adjuster? Do you think anyone will give him a chance to try? Would *you*? His writing is not fraudulent like P's; it's merely pathetic. We can easily imagine hours of bafflement and pencil-chewing, the unsuccessful struggle to answer the demands of an unfamiliar technology. His letter is awkward and inept, like a child's gift of a pencil pot made of Popsicle sticks glued around a soup can, and every bit as revealing of what P would probably call "the uniqueness of a person." That is, not at all. Nevertheless, this poor boy is what our schools have called minimally competent at the very least, and so he will be for the rest of his sad and meager life.

Some useless but interesting questions arise. How much reading did he do as a student of political science and sociology, disciplines not noted for a lack of discursive and theoretical prose? What makes him think that this is how writing is supposed to go? What did his professors say about his writing? Was it with discursive prose like this that he earned his good grades? The questions are useless, of course, because the answers are obvious. Again and again, for all those years of his education, someone

said of his skill, "What the hell, it'll do." To require anything more of him would have been just too much
trouble. Nevertheless, he's one of our successes. Just try
to imagine the failures.

# 15

# Devices
# and Desires

Individual failures will eventually disappear into the morass of the barely educated and barely employable, but corporate failures seem immortal. It is only the failures of the past that the ignorant are condemned to repeat; the successes they are condemned to forget. We are not the first to speak nonsense and to teach it.

When Gulliver went among the Projectors of Lagado, he met some remarkable chaps who were silly linguists but astute prophets. They were looking for a way to escape the constraints of language, and they undertook to do away with words entirely. Since words were, they thought, only names for things, they reasoned that we'd all be better off if we went right to the heart of reality and dealt in the things themselves rather than in the words. They proposed that we might simply carry about with us whatever things might be needful for the conduct of our business. Gulliver had the chance to watch some of them in conversation, setting down their great bundles, pulling forth objects, and holding them up for each other's scrutiny. It's entertaining to imagine them, showing each other egg cups and wrenches and bobby pins and worn-out shoes.

Unfortunately, their noble plan was undone by a coalition of "Women in Conjunction with the Vulgar and the Illiterate," who *will* be nattering in all seasons, and who are always "irreconcilable Enemies to Science." What a pity. Where are those savants now that we need them? Just imagine the benefits that would flow from such a system. Think of the Gross National Product. Think of the factories churning out things, enough things so that every citizen could have a large enough vocabulary to get him through a whole life. Every little child playing on the sidewalks would need at least a large backpack full of stuff. Businessmen would wheel large pushcarts into posh restaurants, and wheeling and dealing would no longer be a metaphor. Scholars would attend conferences in Peoria trailing behind them U-Haul vans full of objects. Yankee ingenuity would quickly provide miniatures of everything imaginable, so that before long you'd be able to discuss the foreign policy of the Carter administration out of one pocket and still have room in another to chat about the weather and complain about inflation. Blissful silence would fall upon the land as people everywhere displayed to each other forks and carburetors and delicate underthings and adorable little models of the Supreme Court Building. Television talk shows would become fascinating exercises in inventiveness, and people would probably buy tickets to watch the chairman of the Federal Reserve trying to explain the rise in the prime rate.

Well, we, of course, are not as silly as the Projectors of Lagado. We are devising far more practical ways to escape the constraints of language. Our substitutes for the logical demands of discursive prose are more subtle, and we have even overcome the traditional enmity of the "Women in Conjunction with the Vulgar and the Illiterate." The women have been convinced that the mastery of discursive prose must wait upon the invention of some new pronouns; the vulgar have been convinced that precision in language is subservience to elitist oppression; and we are now working on ways to convince the illiterate that they're actually better off just watching television.

A contempt of book-learning is not new in America. From some point of view it's even desirable. Those who rule a society and direct its course and devise its laws and control its wealth do so out of certain skills. Our Madisons and Hamiltons and Jeffersons were book-learners. Out of the power of words, they formed a nation to suit their needs, and out of that same power, they governed it. Out of the inescapable implications of their words, they imagined and projected a nation of educated citizens, book-learners, unto whose informed discretion the ultimate authority was to be given. Or so they said. So *we* say. They may have meant it; we don't.

For those who have the power of language, it is a comfort to know that so many others don't. While we keep the powers and privileges that go with skill in language, we are happy to leave the ignorant in what they proudly call the school of hard knocks, sweeping our floors and bruising their knuckles with wrenches. By all means, let them despise book-learning. What do we need with competitors? Book-learning can only lead the multitudes into the ways of knowledge and logical thought, which will make them discontented laborers, undependable voters, and finicky consumers.

Those who can profit from a general anti-intellectualism are the intellectuals, and those who reap the benefits of widespread illiteracy are the literate. The Projectors of Lagado might have succeeded magnificently if they had thought of that. Unfortunately, they took themselves seriously. It's a silly quack who swallows his own snake oil. We are making the same mistake in our academies of projectors. It's one thing to encourage in the ignorant the notion that book-learning is silly and that they don't want any part of it; it's quite another when the book-learners themselves fall for that story.

Here are the words of one of our contemporary projectors. His very title is subtle projection; he is called Learning Resources Center Director. A Learning Resources Center is what we used to call a library, but a library sounds like a dull and solemn place ruled over by scowling spinsters. A Learning Resources Center sounds like a bright and cheery place, shiny with Naugahyde and Formica, where you can get something or other serviced by a smiling attendant. Librarians, furthermore, make us think of books, but Learning Resources Centrists can provide us with filmstrips and 8-track recordings and show us how to work the machines. This particular centrist has concluded that too much fuss is being made about reading and writing and adduces, to support his conclusion, the fact that some films are beautiful and that cassette recorders are very useful for learning foreign languages while driving cars. He says:

More and more colleges and universities in America are admitting students who do not read well, yet most of these same students have a high degree of visual literacy.

They have gained knowledge and understanding through years of exposure to television, films and other image-oriented media. Is the knowledge of these students inferior in quality to the knowledge of their peers who are avid readers?

It would be some comfort to believe that this centrist knew what he was doing. If that were so, we could conclude that he has bought up lots of stock in the electronics industry and that his interesting assertions about gaining knowledge and understanding were designed to increase the sales of video recorders and those cunning devices that permit us to play billiards and blackjack on the screen. Such entertainments must surely provide knowledge and understanding about angles of incidence and reflection and about addition, at least up to twenty-one. Furthermore, if we could be convinced of his astuteness, we could ourselves call our brokers and place a few orders. Unfortunately, however, his language shows us that he has swallowed his own snake oil and that he is not one of the deceivers, whom we would gladly join, but one of the deceived, whom we would like to fleece.

If you cannot be the master of your language, you must be its slave. If you cannot examine your thoughts, you have no choice but to think them, however silly they may be. Had this centrist stopped to examine his language he would have found himself examining his thoughts, and he would have found that they are nonsense. Having bought his own scam, however, he is precluded from such an examination. We are not.

Look first at his reference to "image-oriented media," a modern and trendy term. We know, of course, what "oriented" means, even when it appears in the Illustrated Guide to the Learning Resources Center as "orientated."

If you're oriented, you know which way is east. That much, however, would be of little help to a Bulgarian trying to learn English. He'll be told someday that some people are "print-oriented." Now that does not mean that those people know which way to go to find some print; it means rather that they find print somehow more informative than other things and that they're likely to pay more attention to it than they do even to color pictures of pretty girls with big teeth. While our poor Bulgarian is still trying to decide whether to believe that, he'll hear about something that's "consumer-oriented." He now has to face the hard fact that his understanding of "oriented," even coupled with his understanding of "print-oriented," won't help him with "consumer-oriented." To be "consumer-oriented" does not mean knowing which way to go to find the nearest consumer. It does not mean being more attuned to consumers than to other forms of humanity, misers, for instance. "Consumer-oriented," in fact, can't even be used to describe persons. It goes with whole bureaucracies, maybe, or campaigns, or those little feature items on the women's page in the Sunday paper that are intended to be for the *benefit* of consumers.

Once our Bulgarian has learned about "consumer-oriented," he can go on to tackle something like "success-oriented," which does *not* mean knowing which way success lies, and does *not* mean more likely to be informed by success than by anything else, and does *not* mean providing aid and comfort to success, but *does* mean being impelled in the direction of success. By analogy with "success-oriented," you can say that bombs and bullets are enemy-oriented. But maybe not. "Enemy-oriented" might also mean "designed to serve the needs of the enemy." So be careful.

(This is the final test for jargon: How far can it be

pushed? When that provost told us that his process was made up of components, elements, and factors, we might have been taken in. If we push his jargon far enough and put it into something concrete, like a bologna, for instance, we see that he would have to say that components, elements, and factors were actually the same as slices.)

Having been through all that, can we now understand what he means by the "image-oriented media"? Let's try it with television, which is, by the centrist's admission, one of those media. Does he mean to say that television is pointed in the direction of images and knows how to find them? Does he mean that television seems most comfortable when looking at images? Does he mean that television is an enterprise devoted to the welfare of images? Does he mean that television is motivated by images? Obviously, all of these possibilities are nonsensical. He can only mean that television shows images. That we all knew.

In some ways, being unable to write is like being unable to lie. Evidence betrays the thousands, but ineptitude unmasks the millions. Having caught our centrist in the inanity of "image-oriented media," we have reason to seek out the inanity in "visual literacy" and in that supposed knowledge and understanding that come from long exposure to those "image-oriented media."

Visual literacy. That must be something that comes from looking at images. But wait. The whole universe is an "image-oriented medium." The earth and the sea and the sky and all things everywhere show us images. Alexander the Great saw images all his life; what need had he, then, of Aristotle? Was Ethelred the Unready visually literate through long years of exposure to the world? Or can this visual literacy arise only in those who watch films and television? Must an image be framed in some way before it can produce knowledge and understanding? Are we to believe that a college freshman has "gained" as much knowledge and understanding from watching "Mod Squad" as Galileo from watching the moon? Does the growth of visual literacy require alternating current?

One picture is *not* worth a thousand words. A picture isn't *worth* any words at all. One picture, one glimpse of the moon, even one episode of "Mod Squad," may *cause* a thousand words in some beholder. Or many thousand. Or, in some other beholder, none at all. If knowledge and understanding are to come from watching "Mod Squad" or the moon, they must come in the form of language, the only vehicle we have for knowledge and understanding. Those unfortunate students "who do not read well" may look forever at the moon and have nothing to say, for they have not the power of language, which is why they do not read well. They may have taken something or other from their years of film- and television-watching, but it isn't likely to be knowledge and understanding. Furthermore, whatever knowledge and understanding they found that way came not from the *images* they saw but from some *words* they might have heard. How many of them, do you suppose, were sufficiently "image-oriented" to watch fifteen years of television with the sound turned off?

Let us hope, charitably, that this Learning Resources Center Director never has to fly to a conference in Denver on an airplane designed by a bunch of engineers who "do not read well" but who have, nevertheless, "a high degree of visual literacy." His best hope would be that "visual literacy" is the ability to *see* and *identify* the letters of the alphabet. That, at least, would be some comfort, for it would suggest that the designers of his airplane might have managed to identify slot A and tab A correctly. That way, a bunch of mechanics, also poor readers but visually literate, might just possibly have been able to slip the latter into the former correctly so that the machine will fly for a while.

The centrist asks: "Are colleges and universities routinely to flunk out students who do not learn well from verbally-oriented instruction?" (There's another "oriented," attached this time not to a noun but to an adverb. You'll have to figure that one out for yourself.) And those who can't swim — must they routinely drown when they wander into deep water? And the blind — must they be routinely deprived of driver's licenses?

Of course, the centrist's question isn't quite that simple. The answer depends on just what it is the colleges and universities intend to teach. If they are teaching knowledge and understanding, then it looks bad for those "who do not learn well from verbally-oriented instruction." If they are teaching something else, something which must be utterly inexpressible in language, we have to wonder how they know whether any of the students have learned it. The centrist must want his question answered with the assurance that colleges and universities will routinely *graduate* "students who do not learn well from verbally-oriented instruction," and that, of course, is exactly what they do. Many of these students become teachers, who will provide a never-failing supply of "students who do not learn well from verbally-oriented instruction," so that the centrists of the future will always have a good cause to plead.

The Projectors of Lagado would be delighted with "visual literacy." They didn't have such a nifty name for it, but it's just what they had in mind. After all, when the pretty lady next to you at a dinner party holds up for your consideration a slightly worn head gasket, you do have to be image-oriented enough to *see* what the damned thing is. You do have to have gained lots of knowledge and understanding in order to respond appropriately by showing her a ticket stub and a bent paper clip. Now *that's* communication.

All the zany notions that have corrupted education in the last few decades have some interesting things in common. They have all arisen as education's responses to deficiencies caused by education, and they all promise profit and comfort; the profit to the education industry and the comfort to students and teachers who are given less and less hard work to do. To read a book about geology is tiresome, especially to the unverbally-oriented, or verbally-disoriented, or whatever they are. To watch a little film that shows some sleek cattle grazing within a few yards of the San Andreas Fault is relaxing and humanistic. Furthermore, how much can a geology book cost? Twelve, fifteen dollars at the most. Even a dinky little filmstrip projector costs about ten times as much, and a motion-picture projector, with stereo sound lest the lowing of the cows be dehumanized, costs several hundreds at least. A test on the geology book might present some annoying difficulties, especially for students who aren't too good at reading or writing; but a test on the film would require only that the student admit to having noticed the cows. For a little extra credit, he might assert that the film was handsome and that he appreciated it. As for the teacher, he too is excused from boring reading, although he does have to learn to operate the projector. No problem, that. Schools of teacher training offer numerous courses in the operation of the machines that have transformed libraries into Learning Resources Centers.

We are told, of course, that film projectors and video

recorders and tape machines and all such devices are meant not to replace the printed word but to serve as enlightening adjuncts to books. They certainly can do that. The Learning Resources Center Director, however, doesn't seem to be saying any such thing. He is clearly saying not that students can watch television and film as illustrations to their studies, but that for some students television and films must *be* their study. That would be happy news for the industries that manufacture all those gimmicks.

Those industries will surely have their own motives for encouraging the cause of visual literacy, but we cannot ascribe such crass motives to the educators. Their motives are far less canny, and they arise from a pathetic populism dictated by a sad necessity. This is America, where every child can hope to grow up to be President, or at least a well-paid geologist, say. Imagine an only moderately stupid young man who actually watches "Nova" and thirsts to explore for oil in the service of Exxon. Should he be barred from a respectable trade and deprived of a comfortable income just because he can't read or write or cipher very well? It seems un-American, somehow, that his opportunities should be limited by his abilities. Let's at least give him a chance by showing him some pretty pictures of the walls of the Grand Canyon. We might even get in some actual *oil* and let him smell it and play with it, thus making him not only visually literate but olfactorily and tactilely literate as well. Then we'll graduate him with a degree in geology and let Exxon handle the problem.

The narrow-eyed people at Exxon are, of course, unreconstructed elitists who expect that geologists can read and write and cipher, but that's *their* problem. We are humanistic educators who want everybody to have a chance at everything, and we're not going to be a party to the ruthless elitism of the international energy cartels. And as for the unlucky geology major, currently polishing hubcaps down at the car wash, well, maybe we can talk him into coming back and putting in a couple of years taking courses in education. Then we can get him a certificate as a general science teacher. He ought to be good at showing films and passing around oil. Kids love that kind of thing.

Imagine something even worse: Maybe, just maybe, that poor geology major *wasn't* moderately stupid when he started school. After all, what makes him moderately stupid just now is that he is not at home in the systems by which we express and devise knowledge and meaning. He just can't read and write very well. Is his stupidity innate, or was he given it by a shabby education? Did he fall into the hands of that third-grade teacher and all the others like her? Did *his* general science teacher pass around a can of oil? Were *his* teachers humanistically attuned to the wonders of visual literacy and all that knowledge and understanding to be gained from years of exposure to films and television?

The devices of our loony Projectors are designed to satisfy their own desires. They want to be nice to everybody. They want to be loved. They want to love their work, which is hard to do when the work is demanding and difficult. Having long taught out of these desires, they have raised up to themselves — and to us, worse luck — far more stupid students than Nature would have provided on her own. Now, not oblivious to the plight of these stupid millions, they still want to be nice and, especially, democratic. They want to provide a make-believe education for the unhappy multitudes for whom they have already provided the stupidity that fits them for nothing more than a make-believe education.

It is as though the right hand of Detroit should lose

its cunning and could produce very few automobiles that would actually start, telling us, however, that we would be far better off sitting in our cars in the driveway and playing with the knobs.

And here we sit, pulling on the knobs and twiddling the dials, playing car. The knobs and dials are not connected to anything but it's lots of fun. Nevertheless, this damned thing will never run, and if we want to go anywhere we're going to have to connect these knobs and dials to the machinery. The machinery is there. The language is intact; we're just not hooked up to it.

# 16

# Naming
# and Telling

There is nothing wrong with English. We do not live in the twilight of a dying language. To say that our English is outmoded or corrupted makes as much sense as to say that multiplication has been outmoded by Texas Instruments and corrupted because we've all forgotten the times table. You may say as often as you please that six times seven is forty-five, but arithmetic will not suffer. You, of course, may suffer, and, if you happen to be an aerospace engineer, lots of other people may suffer when your machinery falls into the downtown section of Detroit, but it won't be because of the decay of arithmetic. Those thousands of dead and maimed will not be the victims of a decline in the art of mathematics but simply of ignorance and stupidity, ignorance and stupidity that might have been prevented had you learned to manipulate a system of symbols. If it seems to you that an equivalent error in the symbol system of English can't possibly destroy Detroit, then good luck.

A symbol system that just sits there is no good at all. To learn things, to understand and to predict, we have to manipulate it. The better we manipulate it, the more hope there is for Detroit. No matter how badly we manipulate it, however, it remains what it is — a way of making knowledge and understanding. What is thought to be a decay of English in our time is, in fact, a decay in the brains of those who have not learned to manipulate English. Worms have made their homes in our brains and have eaten away the power of our speech and of our thought. Some highly specialized worms have here and there eaten away the active voice or the prepositional phrase, but the greatest worm of all, the Master Worm, is gnawing away at the Central Control Board, the mechanism that makes language something more than the sum of its parts, the mechanism that links naming and telling.

Consider again that provost who speaks of the elements of the process, and the components of the process, and the factors of the process. He is, of course, being thoughtless and lazy. He is using some more or less right-sounding words to conceal, mostly from himself, the fact that he hasn't thought something out. He just doesn't *know* exactly how to cut up that process and how its various parts are to be related to one another. He is covering the holes in his brain with little slabs of jargon. He has chosen some faddish terms to conceal his failure of thought, but for all the understanding they provide he might just as well have spoken of the segments of the process, or its units, or its compartments. Had he had more time for reflection, we can suspect that he would have spoken of its *essential* elements, its *integral* components, and its factors *to be considered.*

There are plenty of people, most of them in important positions, who write and think like that, covering an emptiness in the brain with jargon. How does that come to pass? The answer is portentous.

It is a special richness of English that it provides its speakers with many long lists of words that mean *nearly* the same thing. Consider the provost's words: element, component, and factor. They all point to a *part* of something. So too do the hypothetical alternatives: segment, unit, compartment. In about two minutes, you should be able to think up eight or nine more words that mean, roughly, a part of something. But only roughly.

In slangs, there are large arrays of synonyms that *do* mean the same thing, because slang is exuberant and poetic. Discursive prose, unfortunately, must be usually sober and precise. Its large arrays of synonyms are designed to provide many slightly different meanings and, accordingly, finer and finer distinctions. To make finer and still finer distinctions is a proper goal of thought. It is the equivalent of making finer and still finer measurements in technology. There is an important difference, however. The fine measurements of technology refer to the world then and there, the world of physical experience; the fine distinctions of language refer to a world that is not *there* in the same sense, but to a world devised in the mind, a world of imaginative construction.

Wouldn't it be interesting to know *exactly* what the provost means by elements, components, and factors? Well, not really; he probably doesn't have any clear idea of what he means. But suppose he did. Then he would be able to explain to us why *this* part of the process is best understood as component while *that* part must be called an element. He would make it clear that the factors of the process are subtly different from the elements and components, and we would behold in wonder an elegant and elaborate construction of the mind of man, a construction that might be useful. But that's not going to happen. In fact, those words, as the provost uses them, are precisely analogous to the synonym lists of slang. Where slang provides a host of colorful names for private parts, the jargon of the provost provides a host of insipid names for any old parts at all. He is reciting a kind of drab doggerel when he pretends to be pursuing thought in discourse.

The business of language is twofold; it is for naming and for telling. Those things are not related to each other in exactly the same way. Telling requires naming, but naming does not require telling. Naming by itself is of little use. Remember the lion in the grass who needs no name. We can, of course, sit around and say to each other the names of nearby things, but that would be an idiotic enterprise suitable for nothing more important than passing the time on a long automobile ride. Speaking our language is not an essay in naming. Speaking our language is a matter of telling, naming things and making propositions about them, which is in effect the arranging of names in such a way as to present for the mind an order of things that is *not* present in the arrangement of things around us. Even words like "when" and "late" are "names" of a sort, but they name relationships and ideas that have no concrete existence in the physical world. Two things, then, are necessary for intelligent discourse: an array of names and a conventional system for telling. The power of a language is related, therefore, to the size and subtlety of its lexicon, its bank of names, and the flexibility and accuracy of its telling system, its grammar. In these respects, English is a tremendously powerful language, and those who know it can do great things and create knowledge and understanding. The trouble with that provost and all the others we have looked at is not that they have corrupted the English language, but that in the fullest sense they don't write the English language. Their naming is insufficient and inaccurate, and their telling is ambiguous and irregular.

In a very complicated culture like ours, there are many things that require extremely precise naming. Even in much simpler cultures there will always be *some* things that require the same. The Eskimos, you will recall, have names for many different kinds of snow, and the Jiukiukwe have names for stones of different shapes. Such distinctions are important parts of their technologies. It seems unlikely, however, that the Eskimos have to devise a complicated set of names for those little tunnels that serve as doorways to their igloos, and the Jiukiukwe, who have no structures at all, need no name for a doorway. Our culture is so complicated that even as simple a thing as a doorway can be an issue in an elaborate technology. That's the reason for that grotesque definition of an exit on page 143. The law is one of our linguistic technologies, and in this case the demands of the law are for precise, complete, and unambiguous meaning. To read such a definition, of course, is no fun, but it isn't really meant to be read. It isn't strictly a piece of writing at all. It isn't "telling" either; it's only a very fussy naming, an extended entry in some imaginable index of special names for special occasions.

Our endless need for new and precise names certainly complicates our language, but such complication doesn't have to cause inanity however much purists may deplore it. Think of the recent adventures of a popular word, "incentive." This word was once a neologism and probably repellent to some, but we have learned to live with it. In fact, we have come to need it, because it makes a precise distinction. To have an incentive is not only to have a reason for doing something, but more specifically to have some hope of profit or advantage from the doing. Indeed, the incentive *is* often the profit or advantage. "Incentive," therefore, is not exactly interchangeable with "motive" or "inducement" or "encouragement," for instance. So what are we to think about a congressman from Pennsylvania who claims to be proud of having invented the word "incentivize," by which he means, of course, "to provide with an incentive"? If you think he has corrupted the English language, try to find a *precise* equivalent, a more traditional naming of exactly that action. To our ears, his word may be ugly, but "incentive" itself was once ugly to the English ear. If "incentivize" names an action that cannot, in fact, be otherwise named, we'll learn to live with it.

In the next chapter of the adventures of "incentive," we hear our Social Security Director speaking of "disincentives" to early retirement. Any right-thinking person recoils in dismay from this hideous word, but a little reflection suggests that it may not be easily replaced with something more familiar. For instance, would "discouragement" do the same job? Not quite. "Discouragement" may be what we feel when we consider how much money it will cost to retire too soon; the "disincentive" is that arrangement in the system that causes the loss of money and the concomitant discouragement.

The making of new names is an inanity only when it isn't necessary. Here again we can see that most of us need to ape those who are higher on the scale of technology. Most of our unnecessary jargon consists of words like "interface" and "input," precise namings at one level of technology, which seep downward into lower levels where they are neither precise nor even needed. There's more to the process, though, than the simple mimicking of somebody else's names; we also mimic the process by which the names come to be made in the first place. That's how we get the inane neologisms like "orientate" and "updation." (That may need clarification for the more sheltered reader: an "updation" is what you get when you are updated. As yet we have no word for what you get when you are dated up. Be patient.) Thus the school people have changed "competence" to "competency," gaining thereby some small increase in self-esteem and a twenty-five percent increase in syllables, but without naming anything that wasn't already named by "competence."

Remember now the prayers of the grant-seekers. If you've forgotten them, here is a mournful reminder: "Within the general system of teaching acts are many subsets of actions and processes." Notice how cunningly this manages to *tell* almost nothing while *naming* many things. All that it *tells* us is that "teaching" has parts, parts that may as well have been called components, elements, and factors. But it *names* a system, even a *general* system as though there were some means to distinguish it from a *specific* system; it names certain acts, here carefully but needlessly distinguished as *teaching* acts; it *names* subsets and actions and processes. It sounds impressive, but it tells nothing.

That was the passage in which we found unspecified but supposedly important "developments in philosophy, psychology, and communications theory." It offered us also "translation, transformation, and organization of subject matter into meanings," a resounding string of names that ought to make certain fine distinctions but don't. In this kind of writing, which must also be called this kind of thinking, the specious elaboration of names becomes so automatic that we find even the unlikely naming of the "instruction of individuals and groups" where the single word "instruction" would have been enough.

It has often been noted that bad English, especially among educators and bureaucrats, is clogged with ponderous parades of nouns: "Government personnel applicants for illiteracy enhancement remediation programs must submit program application permission forms in accordance with bureau application procedure policies," or something like that. Such writing is indeed clogged with nouns, but why? It's simple. Once again, the Master Worm eats away the central switchboard that connects naming to telling. When these people go to say something, they can only babble a string of names.

Now we can understand better the plight of P, whom you will remember as the man who is going to test high school children for minimum competence (or as he would put it, competency) in literacy. He is the man who said:

Our program is designed to enhance the concept of an open-ended learning program with emphasis on a continuum of multi-ethnic, academically enriched learning using the identified intellectually gifted child as the agent or director of his own learning.

Omitting for now his specious modifiers, modifiers that make no useful distinctions, we see that a program is designed to enhance the concept of a program with emphasis on a continuum using a child as an agent or as a director. (It sounds as though those last two might be interchangeable.) This is a failure in the switchboard; telling is overwhelmed by naming. The namings, furthermore, are all abstract, pointing into an evoked world of insubstantial programs and concepts and continua. What, exactly, do we *do* when we enhance the concept of a program? Will emphasis on a continuum do the job? As to the specious modifiers, there too we find naming without telling in a collection of faddish words. Is an open-ended learning program a learning program that is open-ended or is it a program of open-ended learning? Does either of those things make much sense? What other intellectually gifted child than the "identified" gifted child could there possibly be to put into an open-ended learning program or even into a program of open-ended learning? How else but academically might learning be enriched?

If this were a case of telling rather than mere naming, we would have none of those questions. Nevertheless, be mindful of P's problem. He does have to write something once in a while — it's probably in his job description — and there obviously isn't much to tell. He has to say something, and a bewildering exercise in naming may convince the thoughtless and indolent that something must have been told. This is not to say, however, that P is practicing to deceive. The truth is almost surely worse than that. He very probably thinks that he *has* told something and, accordingly, that he has thought something.

Here is a most appropriate example of naming disguised as telling. These are the unconsciously ironic words of some people who imagine that they are going to do something about the writing skills of schoolchildren:

> It is necessary that schools and school districts emphasize the importance of imparting to students the skills and attitudes which are the underpinnings of a comfortable, confident, successful producer of all forms of written matter, including prose, poetry, and practical

narrative and descriptive and interrogatory writing (e.g., letters, applications, requests for information, reports, etc.).

This, after many months of deliberation, was one of the most important conclusions of an advisory committee of experts on reading and writing. They have, in effect, decided that the schools should teach the students how to write. The elevator man, of course, could have told you that. If you don't have an elevator, you could have gotten the same information from the taxi driver or the man who reads the meter. This is by no means to denigrate the achievement of the committee; what has always been perfectly obvious to all the rest of us actually *is* a tremendous breakthrough for educators, and they are much to be congratulated for having so largely transcended their training. However, they have still a little more transcending to do. The passage shows all of the symptoms of profound and probably irreversible brain damage. It could be taken for a miniature model of everything that is seriously wrong with the use of English in our time. Reading prose like that is like watching some game in which you can't see the ball.

Give yourself a little test. Don't reread the passage. It is, although it probably didn't seem so when you read it, all one sentence. Try hard to remember the subject of the sentence. The subject of a sentence is not just a grammatical reality; it is a reality of thought. It's what the sentence is about, or, in more appropriate terms right now, it is the "naming" at the heart of the "telling." If you have been able to remember the subject, you should have no trouble remembering the verb, and when you do you will have recalled the very core of this sentence, the hard, inner skeleton of meaning so characteristic of sentences in English and many other languages. In this case, however, the skeleton is a little squishy: It is "It is."

Where this writer says "It is necessary that the schools" and so forth, you or I or the elevator man would probably say: "The schools should do something." Even so, we would only be trying to make the best of the bad mess. Is this sentence supposed to be about *schools?* Or is it supposed to be about *writing?* "It" is only the grammatical subject of the sentence; what the sentence is *about* is unclear. The schools and school districts, along with a whole catalogue of other things, have been submerged into a "that" clause. This is another way of evading responsibility and pointing not to what is in the mind of the writer but to what we're supposed to understand, apparently, as a condition in the universe. The writer is putting as much distance as possible between himself and what he says. Such prose is a form of immorality, similar to the Divine Passive and the dangling modifiers of the chair of the EEOC. People who write like that are in flight from the responsibility implied by the basic structure of the English in which doers do deeds.

Prose that clouds responsibility also diminishes humanity. When Churchill said, "We shall fight on the beaches," his grammar said for him, and to all of us who share that grammar: "I, a man, speak these words out of the thoughts of my mind, and I mean them." Suppose that he had said instead: "It may become necessary that we fight on the beaches." *Then* his grammar would have said for him and to us: "There may be in the universe some condition of which we ought to be mindful. You will understand, of course, that this is what should be said, but as to whether or not the whole thing is my idea or not is neither here nor there." Englishmen might well have packed up by the millions and moved to Nova

Scotia. The writer of our passage would probably have said: "It may become necessary that we emphasize the importance of imparting to ourselves the skills and attitudes which are the necessary underpinnings of successful engagers in all forms of combat on the beaches." Englishmen are plucky, but not that plucky. After such words they would simply have surrendered.

Naming without telling is equally an evasion of responsibility. We can talk about components, elements, factors, sets, subsets, translations, and transformations only because we do not expect to be called to account for our words. The more of these words we use, the better we can bewilder the reader or even bamboozle him into the conviction that we must know what we are talking about, thus putting off, perhaps forever, the day of reckoning. Notice how that happens in the passage just cited. What should the schools — *and* the school districts — actually do? They should emphasize. That's what it says — that's the verb that goes with the schools and the school districts. And what should they emphasize? They should emphasize importance. Importance? What importance should they emphasize? They should emphasize the importance of imparting! Can we ask "imparting what?"? No, not yet. First we must ask "imparting to whom?" So we ask it. We are answered that they should emphasize the importance of imparting to *students*. Ah! All of a sudden some human beings appear. Unfortunately, however, they will turn out to be superfluous, because there just isn't anyone around in the schools and school districts *except* students to whom to *do* that imparting whose importance is to be emphasized. So we go on. Now we can ask "imparting what?" Imparting skills and attitudes, of course. What skills and attitudes? Skills and attitudes which are underpinnings, naturally. Underpinnings of a producer. What else did you expect? What kind of a producer? A comfortable, confident, successful producer. And so on. The thirty-fourth and thirty-fifth words of this sentence are "written matter."

Someone here has taken great pains *not* to say something. Even "writing" is avoided. We hear, instead, about "written matter," which presumably includes clay tablets and the "Hot" and "Cold" labels on faucets. "Written matter" is needlessly, but meagerly, elaborated into "prose, poetry, and practical narrative and descriptive and interrogatory writing," to say nothing of the e.g. This is one of those catalogues of names meant to convince the reader that somebody has thought all this out. Unfortunately, the silly invention of "interrogatory writing" gives the game away and reveals that these are all names, not thoughts, and that nothing is told.

When the connections between naming and telling are broken, our language becomes subhuman. The crows and the antelope exist by a system of reflexive naming, a sort of sublanguage perfectly suited to serve the needs of herds and flocks. That sublanguage, not surprisingly therefore, flourishes most where we have formed our own herds and flocks, in bureaucracies and corporate structures. Some individual human being wrote that stuff about emphasizing the importance of imparting. Lost somewhere in that producer's underpinnings, there is a human mind with the power of rational thought. What has become of it? Where is Nigger Jim, now that we need him? He would ask: Is a bureaucrat a man? Is an educationist a man? How come he don't speak like a man?

# 17

## Sentimental Education

We Americans are wondrously religious, or at least apocalyptic. We believe that the meaning of things is to be seen not in the way things are but in the way they will be someday. When the urgings of evidence suggest that we are in trouble, we are untroubled, because we are still, and always, on our way. We hate stupidity and ignorance, of course, but we know that they're only temporary. Although stupidity and ignorance are not rare and although they don't seem to be diminishing, we do not characterize America as a nation of stupid and ignorant people. It's the same with things like crime and poverty and racial hatred. Well, yes, we *have* those things, and, yes, they do seem to be growing, but that doesn't mean that America is a nation of criminals and paupers and bigots. There *are* such people, but they are aberrations. In time we'll change all that. Education — that's the answer to it all.

Education will wipe out stupidity and ignorance. Informed and intelligent people will know better than to stick up gas stations for a lousy thirty bucks. They will have the skills to make good honest livings, mostly as chairmen of the boards of General Motors or IBM. As we learn more about each other, black, white, brown, whatever, we'll find new respect for each other and new values in the mingling of our variously rich cultures, and the black and the brown faces will be seen not only in the halls of Congress and the faculties of our venerable universities and colleges but even on hockey teams. Now that's the real America, look, right over there, you have to squint a little, see, there just above that fruited plain?

The history of mankind hasn't yet provided any examples of a decrease in stupidity and ignorance and their presumably attendant evils, but we have hope. After all, history hasn't provided anything like us, either, until pretty recently. The American experiment is unique, especially the American experiment in education. It is that which accounts for our amazing progress and the effectiveness of our technology. We educate (well, we're *going* to educate, just you wait and see) *all* the people, not just the upper classes, not just the specialists, not *any* fraction of any kind, but everybody. History doesn't scare us. We are the Americans.

But even for the Americans the swift eradication of stupidity and ignorance is a large undertaking. Let's not think about all of that just now. Let's imagine something smaller and try to foresee its consequences. Let's simply ask what it would take to provide all the third graders in America with teachers who are correct and precise in their spelling and punctuation. After all, that's not an unreasonable expectation. Spelling and punctuation can be learned, and teachers, of all people, can be expected to have learned them. So what must we do?

First, let's be reasonable. Anyone who writes English

makes an occasional little mistake in spelling. We won't insist on absolute accuracy at all times, but somewhere between absolute accuracy at all times and four appearances of "artical" in a short public letter we must draw a line. It seems reasonable to draw that line somewhat closer to accuracy than to "artical." Are our teachers the hope of the nation? Well, of course. Are they the leaders of our youth into the paths of knowledge and the exercise of the mind? You know it. At those little academic skills like spelling and punctuation should they be as good as the average American? No, better. Better than three quarters of us all? At the least. Better than nine out of ten? That seems reasonable. Pick any number you like.

The simplest and most drastic way to achieve that result would be to give all third-grade teachers a test and send away into the Peace Corps in Afghanistan any who can't spell and punctuate. Could we do this? Certainly not. Someone will show that the test is culturally biased against those in whose background there can be shown a distinct distaste for spelling, which is, after all, nothing more than a genteel skill prized mostly among idle ladies of the privileged classes, like painting on velvet. The testing of teachers is not encouraged by teachers' organizations. It is their view, anyway, that a teacher's competence is demonstrated by the granting of a certificate.

That moves us back a square. Perhaps we can arrange that those who grant those certificates will withhold them from incipient third-grade teachers until they have passed the spelling and punctuation test. If you happen to be an idle lady of the privileged classes and tired of painting on velvet, you can find a new and exciting hobby by writing to certifying agencies and state boards of education and legislators and urging some such thing. Eventually, you'll be able to fill whole scrapbooks with entertaining replies and perhaps even strike a deal with some publisher of humorous paperbacks. You'll be told that the certifiers certify whomsoever the teacher-training academies put forth as certifiable. You may even be told that, whatever evidence you may have to the contrary, third-grade teachers certainly do know how to spell and punctuate, since those teacher-training academies have the highest standards and would never put forth as a candidate for certification anyone lacking such basic skills. The love between the certifiers and the teacher-training academies is warm and undying. The certifiers in no way construe their task as "checking up" on the productions of the teacher trainers.

So we move back one more square and call on the dean of the local teacher-training academy. He greets us warmly and offers us seats and instant coffee with Popsicle-stick stirrers. He (well, perhaps he's a he/she) is always glad to contribute to an increased awareness on the part of the public of issues and concerns centered around the question of current practices in the field of education. He will assure us of the commitment "on the part of I and my colleagues" to excellence and professionalism, including the mastery of skills/methods relevant to desirable outcomes. He will assure us that trained observers have, in the case of each candidate for certification, observed and made judgments upon several dimensions of behaviors and that interaction analysis, as studies have shown, confirms that student teachers can be seen to have demonstrated practical/theoretical sensitization to certain desirable teaching actions and procedures, and that he is perfectly satisfied that instruments already administered tend to corroborate these findings. We feel that we would like to administer unto *him* some instrument, but we restrain ourselves and persist in asking about spelling and punctuation. He reminds us of the affective and non-cognitive parameters and points out that basic language arts competencies are in the charge of another department. But surely, we ask, the teacher-teachers will notice from time to time that some would-be teacher can't spell or punctuate. Now we learn that teacher-teachers are interested in things like their students' positive self-images and their ability to identify with members of other cultures and their effectiveness in maintaining an even temperature in the classroom at all times. Furthermore, we learn that much of the teaching of teachers is accomplished by breaking up into small groups and discussing issues/concerns relative to preassessment without much attention to mechanical details like spelling and punctuation.

There's no help for it. We go back another square to the people who *are* in charge of spelling and punctuation, only to learn that they don't see it that way. Not many of those who teach the freshman composition course are still mired in the outworn age of print, or, as they put it, the print media. Most of their students are into communications media or even multimedia communications. There are some courses in *creative* writing but creative writing does not concern itself much with spelling and punctuation. Furthermore, even should some would-be third-grade teacher find herself in a writing course, and even should she prove unable to spell or punctuate, the final judgment of her language arts competency would be made not on the basis of merely mechanical considerations but rather as a result of the earnestness of her endeavor and the originality of her ideas. Besides, this is a college, and if students come to us from high schools where they are not taught spelling and punctuation, there's nothing we can do about it. If we limited our enrollments to those who *can* spell and punctuate, we wouldn't be able to pay for the electricity to run our multimedia machines and we'd be hauled into court for discriminating against whole legions of minorities, including would-be third-grade teachers whose consciousnesses have been raised to that point where they just know that we are trying to exclude them from a respectable and not-too-demanding profession on nothing more than the flimsy pretext that they are unable to punctuate or spell, overlooking entirely the fact that they just love children.

So we go backward square by square. The principal of the high school refers us to the principal of the junior high school who refers us to the principal of the elementary school. Here, at the bitter end, we hear the worst news of all. Here we are told: Yes, it's true. We do have some trouble teaching spelling and punctuation. But what can we do? Why, the third-grade teachers themselves have some trouble with those things. And there we are, staring into an infinite regression. We cannot raise up unto ourselves a generation of third-grade teachers who can spell and punctuate until we first provide ourselves with a generation of third-grade teachers who can spell and punctuate. The problem isn't here and it isn't there; it's everywhere. If we want to do only so simple a thing as ensure that all third-grade teachers will be expert in spelling and punctuation, we will have to change everything that happens at every step of the process by which we now provide ourselves with third-grade teachers. Lacking such unimaginably large changes, we must simply reconcile ourselves to third-grade teachers whose spelling and punctuation are just a little bit shabby.

If we could make those changes, however, we would find that we had also dealt with the executive secretary, and the provost, and the entire bureaucracy of the Department of Transportation, and even the president of the University of Arizona. They all come from the same litter. They are all examples of an education that does not foster precision and correctness. It's not that that education is *unable* to foster precision and correctness, for in some cases and in some degree it *does* do that. It can be done, most easily, through study and practice in the arts of language and number. We know how to do it. We have chosen not to do it and, having so chosen, have by now brought ourselves to that extremity from which we cannot turn back without turning everything over.

We are in some danger. It is with us as it is with a man who has chosen to play at once upon the ukulele and the harmonica while standing on one foot on the tip of a Coke bottle and twirling on the other foot two Hula-Hoops and spinning a platter on the end of a long stick balanced on his nose. His act may be ill-advised, but this is not the time to discuss it with him. What we do is incalculably more complicated and difficult than any juggling act, and, lacking hope of swift and total destruction, there's obviously no end to it. We can never stop and take a bow. Well, we could stop, but we wouldn't be in any condition to bow, and it is doubtful that anyone would applaud.

Collectively, we own and operate an enterprise complicated far beyond the power of any single mind to grasp in its entirety. We manufacture, by millions and billions, complicated and cunning devices beyond the dreams even of our grandparents. We operate massive, interlocking systems and actually keep track of billions, perhaps trillions, of bits of information. The successes of our systems are staggering. The banks do keep track of our accounts. We punch some buttons and find ourselves talking to a librarian in Athens if we please. Great contraptions of metal, bigger than some garden-style apartment houses, do get into the air and fly to Copenhagen, and the innumerable pages of the Sunday *New York Times* are covered with print every week as long as there isn't a strike. That's not all. When it says that a story is continued on page 43, it usually is.

Nevertheless, there are signs of trouble. Somebody keeps losing enriched plutonium and even gold bullion. The latter will probably make its way harmlessly to a numbered account in Switzerland, but the former may well make its way to the IRA or the PLO. In some cars somebody has been putting the wrong engine, and other cars are cunningly designed to explode on impact. If your car doesn't explode, maybe your tires will. Deadly substances seep from the earth under the swing sets in the backyards of innocent home owners. A keypunch operator punches the wrong key and sends you 436 subscriptions to *Poultry Gazette*, and another keypunch operator deposits an extra $30,000 in your checking account, which seems grand until the IRS starts asking you to account for it. You discover that it is no longer humanly possible to change an erroneous bill from the gas company. A Christmas card from your great-aunt arrives three and a half years late, and the freight car bringing your new trash compacter has disappeared somewhere on a siding in Nebraska. It looks as though things are beginning to fall apart.

Those are only the things that we know about. We do not know what critical matter has gone awry in the State Department or what mistaken conclusions based on false logic and insufficient information have been formed in the Pentagon. We do not know that our surgeon has been shown the wrong lab reports, lab reports in any case misleading because the lab technician has added instead of subtracted, and we do not know that the nurse has given us somebody else's name tag. All of our systems seem to be outgrowing our abilities to deal with them.

It may be that we have not done well to build such colossal complexities into our culture. It may be that the Jiukiukwe do live "better" than we in some way, in simple peace, but they also live miserably, and it's far too late to opt for the simple life. If we drop the Hula-Hoops, the platter will crash down on our heads and we'll break the ukulele and choke on the harmonica, to say nothing of what will happen when we land on the Coke bottle. We must keep the damned thing going, and that requires intelligent thought and the habit of precision.

I once visited a large military base where recruits were trained by the thousands. Most of it was unenlightening, except for the parachute-packing school, which was amazing. Young men, *very* young men, were busy learning to fold and tuck and arrange acres of cloth and miles of cord. A taciturn and unentertainable master sergeant was showing me around. He hadn't smiled when I asked him to show me the ropes, and he didn't smile when I asked him how on earth they tested the work of the parachute packers to find out whether or not they had passed the course. Simple, he said. The student would pack a few parachutes and the instructor would choose one at random, the one that the student would use when he jumped out of an airplane right after lunch. It was easy to tell who had passed and who had failed.

Parachute-packing isn't all that hard. Although it does require the habit of precision, as well as some small manual dexterity, it calls for little intelligent thought, and fairly stupid recruits learn it without much difficulty. However stupid they may be, they are surely what an educationist would call "highly motivated." Now if a couple of callow noncoms can teach a pimply dropout to pack a parachute as though his life depended on it, why is it that sixteen years of schooling cannot teach a third-grade teacher to spell?

Spelling isn't all that hard, either. If the United States Army or AT&T, for that matter, were to decide that its people had to spell correctly, then they would find ways to teach spelling, and the people would learn. Industries, especially, are doing something very much like that already. They find more and more that whatever skills they had hoped to find in college graduates must, in fact, be taught after graduation. Where great expertise is required in certain technical callings, industries often have not only to teach all their people but also to obliterate the ineptitudes and misinformation they got in college. Fewer and fewer courses of study actually prepare people for careers. When they are at their best, they prepare people to prepare for careers.

It could be worse. Many of our college graduates *are* at least prepared to prepare for a career and thus able to learn on the job how to do the job correctly and effectively. Would-be journalists and accountants and engineers learn that there *is* a life after college, because after four years of more or less social promotion they find themselves on a sterner testing ground. Now they *must* learn accuracy and correctness or look for another way of life, perhaps as salesmen of shoes. Exxon will not for long keep paying the would-be geologist solely because he loves oil and tries very hard. The incipient teacher, however, *will* be retained — permanently — if he "really cares" about children and tries very hard. When the brand-new physician is handed his license to practice, the testing of his competence begins. When the brand-new teacher is given his certificate, the testing of his intellectual competence is over. From now on he will be tested only in other matters: his ability to get along with assistant principals and guidance counselors, his dress and deportment, and the tranquillity of his classroom. Unless he is visibly and outrageously ignorant and illiterate, no one will ever again assess the work of his mind. Or, more precisely, no one *within that system* will assess the work of his mind. That's not considered professional and would set a very dangerous example.

From the center of our civilization — our system of education, the largest single enterprise we have — the fog of thoughtlessness and imprecision spreads in all directions. People who cannot get their thoughts straight through the control of language live baffled and frustrated lives. They must accept stock answers to their most vexing questions; they are easily persuaded by flawed logic; they cannot solve their problems because they cannot express them accurately. Worst of all, they cannot even discern their plight, for to do so requires a kind of "discerning" of a world not present to immediate experience, a world that "exists" only in the discourse that they have not mastered.

Pity that chair, a lady beset by what must be a demanding and unhappy task. The EEOC, after all, is mostly a massive complaint department, and the complaints brought to it, trivial as some might seem, are of tremendous importance to certain human beings and worthy of respect and intelligent attention. What a job it must be. It requires not only a well-formulated understanding of humanity but a thorough knowledge of many laws, rules, regulations, and the continuous application of logical thought informed by fact. When we looked at the language of the chair, we were driven to conclude that one of two things must be true. Her distortions of English could be seen either as "mistakes," in which case her education seemed inadequate to her task, or as unconscious revelations of an unspoken feeling about her work and the people for whom she works. It must be, in fact, that both of these things are true.

To do that work, even for a master of the technology of thought, would be difficult and discouraging. How easy it must be, but still how unpardonable, to blame the pains and frustrations of the work on those exasperating citizens who *will* be complaining and mistreating each other in all seasons. When we combine the chair's obviously indifferent education with the inescapable anguish of her work, we cannot be surprised that her language betrays her and evokes a world that is not, a world that suits her far better than the world we count on her to understand and manipulate. She is come into deep waters where she cannot stand. Yet that work must be done.

While we require in tens of millions the habit of precision, in other millions we require as well the further and even more important ability that flows from the careful use of language — the power of thought in discourse. How many chairs of how many commissions are there who lack that power because of sloppy language? How many precise thinkers do we need? Where will we get them? Is there some number below which we cannot fall if chaos is to be postponed yet another year? Are we approaching that number? What can we say of our campaign to wipe out stupidity and ignorance when we see that so many who are paid for the work of their minds wander in darkness and fog?

To dispel ignorance, of course, is only the second aim of education; the first aim is to overcome stupidity. Stupidity is the natural condition of mankind, and if we just left ourselves alone most of us would be stupid. It's like teeth.

Without dentistry, most of us would have crumbling and crooked teeth, and those few naturally endowed with tough enamel and a good bite would become an envied elite, happily savaging steaks and chops while the rest of us sit around gumming stews and porridge.

The ordinary stupidity of mankind can be cured or at least severely mitigated. It isn't even especially difficult to do. Intelligence is, after all, not so much an innate propensity as an invention, a device designed and elaborated mostly for technological purposes. Intelligence can be understood as a learned system for distinguishing between things that seem similar and discovering the similarities in things that seem different. Stupidity is the lack of such a system. We can teach intelligence to the stupid just as easily as we can straighten crooked teeth, but we do have to *do* it. It doesn't just happen. To make the stupid intelligent requires little more than skill and practice in language.

There are other symbol systems in which to practice intelligence. Mathematics and physics and perhaps even music seem to be systems for the uttering of propositions and the exploration of likeness and difference, but they are obviously less accessible to most of us than the language we all learn to speak. It may be that the propensities for learning those symbol systems simply aren't to be found in most of us any more than tough enamel, but the propensities for language are universal, and only in special and pathological conditions do human beings fail to learn a language.

However, while language is the most readily available device for the work of intelligence, just to know a language is not enough any more than being able to wiggle your fingers is enough to make you a pianist. For most of us, the rudimentary skills of language we all have even before we go to school are to intelligent discourse what "Chopsticks" is to music. The aim of education is to make those rudimentary skills into the medium of thought.

The possession of language, like the fact of birth, makes us human beings. Neither the language nor the birth is by itself enough to make us civilized human beings. Civilization develops in us, one by one, in a process that often seems analogous to the growth of civilization in mankind at large. We begin as brutes, cute brutes maybe, but brutes. We become barbarians. Eventually, sometimes, we become civilized members of a complicated technological culture. Civilization, whether individual or collective, grows as ideas are constructed in coherent discourse. As things stand with us just now, we are ready to count it a success should we be able to convert some number of brutes into barbarians.

This kind of book traditionally concludes with an earnest little sermon made up of helpful hints. I have none to offer. I can offer only the reasons that seem to preclude helpful hints.

1. There is literacy and there is literacy. The ability to do some reading and to do some writing is a kind of literacy, to be sure, but it is the kind of literacy that might have been attained three thousand years ago before the invention of discursive prose and the birth of formal reasoning. Meager as that literacy may be, it is the kind of literacy that we haven't been able to achieve, since it is the very goal of such social disorders as the Plain English Fad and the Minimum Competence Mania. The elaborate and technological civilization that we must operate calls for much more than that. It requires millions of people able to construct and follow discursive thought. It demands widespread competence in little things as well

as great, habits of precision, to be learned only through a mastery of the symbol system of language. For many reasons, it has become more and more difficult to teach that greater literacy, and we have chosen to settle for the lesser. We're not doing too well at that. Every year, as our civilization grows more complex, that lesser literacy becomes less and less adequate, and greater and greater multitudes of people are left behind in a fog of ineffectiveness. As those multitudes grow, it becomes more and more difficult to teach even that lesser literacy, which must, accordingly, grow always less. And the time must come, therefore, when very few of us will have the skills with which to construct and follow discursive thought. We will rule the land, but it will not be a restful occupation or a long-lasting one.

2. All of that might be avoided only through a massive change in our system of public education, perhaps only through its annihilation and total reconstruction. Education as now constituted will never do more than the least it can do. The reason for that is easy to see. Of all of the elaborate corporate institutions in our civilization, education is the only one in which there is no important incentive to success. Educators do not even have to bother their heads about getting reelected. The prosperity of the schools does not depend on successful schooling. Indeed, in the current hysteria over the obvious failures of the schools, we have chosen to send good money after bad and enrich our schools in direct proportion to their failures. This further makes it seem likely that should the schools actually succeed, all they could expect would be the withdrawal of the enrichment that comes with failure. That must be what is meant by a "disincentive."

For the individuals in public education, there *are* incentives to success, but they have almost nothing to do with the teaching of students. The successful members of the system are those who can escape the tedious demands of the classroom. From that escape, talented and effective teachers are generally debarred, partly because they are little likely to seek it and partly because of a reasonable institutional bias against removing a good teacher from the classroom. As a result, and in spite of the sentimental folklore of the trade, there are in fact no significant rewards available to the good teacher. Nor are there any significant punishments for the bad teacher. Indeed, it is the bad teacher who is the more inclined and encouraged to escape the classroom and thus achieve what is recognized as a success in public education, an administrative position. The making of policy, therefore, is ultimately given over to the least competent individuals in the system.

3. Public education is dreary. It is dreary because it is boring. It is boring because it requires of its captives only a small portion of their attention, leaving the better part of their energies unfocused. That is why the first concern of parents, teachers, and administrators is for what they call "discipline." The schools have become dangerous places, but that is partly their own doing. They respond to the problem of "discipline" by calling for the restraint and punishment of the unruly; restraint and punishment, however, will provide not discipline but, at the best, a temporary and sullen obedience. Ruly behavior expresses a ruly mind, and the discipline of word and thought provides the discipline of deed. From those incarcerated in enforced idleness, discipline cannot be expected. A rigorous course of study in mathematics or Latin will engender more discipline than a thousand guards, but the system is able to provide only the latter.

4. The supposed American commitment to universal

public education is, in fact, nothing more than a congregational recitation of unexamined slogans. We do not know what we *mean* by an education, because we have not examined the language in which we describe it. We have not examined that language because we are not in the habit of examining language. We are not in that habit because we have been corporately educated in a system in which the critical examination of language and the skills required for that examination are less and less taught. They are less and less taught because they are less and less to be found among those who teach and those who direct the course of education. They are less and less to be found because people who do have the skills of critical thought and clear language are not likely to waste them by going to work in an institution founded on the recitation of unexamined slogans.

It takes some kind of a fool to spend his life in the maximization of potential through the application of sets and subsets of actions aimed at the translation, transformation, and organization of matter into meaning for individuals and groups. Only the thoughtless can pompously tell themselves about things like behavior modification and catalytical non-disciplines and preassessment instruments. No one skilled in language and thought could keep his sanity in that world of empty jargon, where he would find himself set to the task of pretending to clarify fictitious values and enhancing the self-esteem of the utterly unskilled by preaching that a positive self-image is more important than a clear sentence. In short, the land of public education provides a happy home only for those in whom the skills of language and thought are but poorly developed. When linguistically skilled persons do wander into that world, they must soon either leave it or withdraw into the privacy of their own classrooms and learn to ignore everything else. They are strangers in a strange land where the natives speak no rational tongue at all.

The absence of a rational language is necessary to the peace of that system. Its *lingua franca* of unreason provides pretended answers to the questions we might ask about incentive. Just *why* do you want to succeed in teaching the young? we ask. They answer: Because we are professionals committed to excellence and quality education. What is "quality education"? Here are the answers of a widely read educationist. It is an education in which

> . . . students are taught to appreciate . . . cultures other than their own and to perceive themselves in a positive light. In addition, they are encouraged to express their feelings openly and honestly, to develop and maintain good interpersonal relationships and to question basic ideas.

These empty slogans were put forth in defense of the schools against the charge of failing to teach elementary skills of reading and writing. In what language then will those students "question basic ideas"? How will they know them when they see them? Will they ever question the basic ideas implicit in "appreciating" cultures and perceiving themselves in "positive lights"? These are not, it is important to note, the words of an eccentric educationist swimming against the tide. They express the orthodox creed. The robe of education in our time is a scanty garment; most of it is lunatic fringe.

A line runs from the meditations of the heart to the words of the mouth. The meditations are not clear to us until the mouth utters its words. If what the mouth utters is unclear or foolish or mendacious, it must be that the meditations are the same. But the line runs both ways. The words of the mouth will *become* the meditations of the heart, and the habit of loose talk loosens the fastenings of our understanding.

Sometimes we all know that. When a functionary of our government tells us that his previous statements have suddenly become "inoperative," we see that what has been committed is not a euphemism but an immorality. While pretending to admit to the truth, the word evokes a world that never was, a world in which sentences that were once "true" now become, through some random twitch of history, not exactly "false" but at least ineffective, like an engine that used to start but doesn't anymore now that the weather has turned cold. We may snicker and even sneer at the man who tells us that his words have now become "inoperative," but he still has a victory. He has put that tiny worm into our ears. It will eat its way into our brains and dull some power of language, so that when his successors later talk to us about "enhanced radiation devices" we may sneer and snicker less. When enough of those worms have made their homes in our skulls — how long do you suppose that will take? — the day will come when we merely nod.

And from nodding we will go to dozing, and from dozing, to sleep.

# Critical
# Bibliography

It's hard to know what to call the citations that I have used in this book. Except for a few minor entries — the imagined beginnings of some memos and letters and the facetious but not unlikely grant proposal — they were all written by human beings in the course of their labors. I would like to characterize them, therefore, as "real," but somehow the word seems to suggest either too much or not enough. They *are* real, real writings of real people, to be sure, and real pieces of paper bearing real bunches of marks, and yet to call them "real" and to leave it at that seems at least a mild abuse of language. Authentic? Genuine? I just don't know. Let it be. Real they are, and yet unreal.

The chair of the EEOC is, of course, the real chair of the real EEOC, and her words are taken from an article purporting to describe a "reform" of some kind in that agency. Her writing should make us wonder just what sort of reform we can expect. Could clients and charging parties be eliminated as effectively in fact as they are in grammar, the work of the EEOC would surely diminish. That would be, I suppose, a kind of reform.

The third-grade teacher, of course, is a real third-grade teacher, and the teacher candidates who are quoted at length in Chapter 8 are every bit as real as she. Furthermore, those candidates must have been doing their very best. Those little scraps of writing were done in the hope of gainful employment. In the text, I have called them "essays," but they aren't any such thing. They are disorganized and ill-remembered recitations; an essay is a weighing and testing of thought and idea in discourse. "Essaying" is a trying-out; these little scraps are trottings-out.

The provost at least used to be real. He may still be real, but he is no longer a real provost. He was the chief academic officer of a large branch of a large state university. His departure from provosthood seems not to have been because of his language. Inane language has never blighted an academic career.

The forester was, of course, applying for a grant. He wanted — and who can blame him — to wander around in the woods at our expense, stopping awhile here and there and saying, "Gee, wouldn't this be a great place for some picnic tables." So what could the poor fellow do? If he had put it that way, no one would have shelled out tax money, so he had to talk about sub-variables and the existing physical status. For *that* we give money. I know another woodland wanderer who says, in his Ph.D. dissertation: "The purpose of this section is to examine part of the valley infrastructure of seemingly vital importance to the success of the Project as a recreation facility: accessibility by recreationists." I will considerately say no more of him, except to assure you that he got his degree and a choice appointment. I like to imagine these two outdoor types meeting by the shores of a mountain lake and exchanging views. The one would speak lyrically of groupings, both physical and socio-economic, and the other would urge "ground-truthing," one of his favorite activities.

The definition of teaching as a "systematic series of actions directed toward specific ends" has an interesting provenance. Who wrote it I don't know. It was put forth with the boast that thirteen people had labored for eighty hours to produce it. That's one thousand forty hours, and the laborers were all highly paid educationists, so the document must have cost much more than seven maids with seven mops for half a year. Neither group could get it clear. Sad to say, the passage is from a proposal to establish a program for the training of excellent teachers.

The dervish of Chapter 11 is also real, although he makes that word sound even less appropriate. The stuff that he writes he also teaches, at public expense, in a state college in the Northwest. Some people have found his work so ludicrous that they thought it must have been made up by me. Impossible. Some kinds of bad language can be faked, since they are rigidly formulaic, but only a true believer can dream up on-site/off-site, bipolar, entities and dyads. If you find yourself laughing at this writer, try to remember that every two weeks when he picks up his paycheck the laugh is on you. If it would make you feel better to imagine that he is the only one of his kind in American education, go ahead and try.

The words of P were chosen because they ought to be familiar by now. Unlike the other examples, they have been widely quoted in the public press. P is, maybe was, a high school principal in Texas. P's companion in misery, the young man who wants to be an insurance adjuster, is, maybe was, also real, a recent graduate of a middle-sized middle Atlantic university. I wonder where he is now.

The Learning Resources Centrist does his centering in the South in a prestigious institution of higher learning. (They do call themselves "centrists" sometimes, but it seems to me that a centrist, like a communist or formalist, ought to be not one who *does* something about centers or centering, but one who is committed to the principles of centers or centering. Well, no matter.) His letter was, in fact, an objection to my objection to the term Learning Resources Center for library.

The educationist quoted in the last chapter, and also in the context of "values clarification," is a professor of educational psychology in Southern California. "Educational psychology" is possible in language, so why not in Southern California?

The source of the other citations is suggested in the text.

I should say, for those who might think these things unusual, that they aren't and that they weren't difficult to find. They were chosen from among hundreds of possible examples, almost any selection of which could have been used to make the same point. Especially in education, government, psychology, and the social sciences, but to some degree in every sort of thoughtful endeavor, such writings are not exceptions; they are the rule. They also suggest the rule under which we must all live someday unless something changes.